KU-052-706

LOUIS MacNEICE
AND THE POETRY OF THE 1930s

Richard Danson Brown

NORTHCOTE
BRITISH COUNCIL

For my family: Pat, Chris, Neil, Jean and Jonathan

© Copyright 2009 by Richard Danson Brown

First published in 2009 by Northcote House Publishers Ltd, Horndon, Tavistock, Devon, PL19 9NQ, United Kingdom.
Tel: +44 (0) 1822 810066 Fax: +44 (0) 1822 810034.

All rights reserved. No part of this work may be reproduced or stored in an information retrieval system (other than short extracts for the purposes of review) without the express permission of the Publishers given in writing.

British Library Cataloguing-in-Publication Data
A catalogue record for this book is available from the British Library

ISBN 978-0-7463-1180-6 hard cover
ISBN 978-0-7463-1185-1 paperback

Typeset by PDQ Typesetting, Newcastle-under-Lyme
Printed and bound in the United Kingdom

WITHDRAWN FROM STOCK
SWANSEA LIBRARY UNIVERSITY

Contents

Acknowledgements

Grateful acknowledgement is made to the following sources:

N. Cameron, 'Nostalgia for Death', in *Collected Poems and Selected Translations*, ed. W. Hope and J. Barker (Anvil Press, 1990).

C. Day Lewis 'Conflict' and 'Learning to Talk', in *A Time to Dance and Other Poems* (Hogarth Press, 1935).

Various material by Louis MacNeice used by permission of David Higham Associates.

P. Muldoon, '7, Middagh Street', in *Poems 1968–1998* (Faber & Faber and Farrar, Straus and Giroux, 2001), LLC.

Various material from S. Spender in *New Collected Poems*, ed. M. Brett, Faber & Faber © 2004, reprinted by kind permission of the Estate of Sir Stephen Spender.

Every effort has been made to trace copyright owners, but if any have been inadvertently overlooked, the publishers will be pleased to make the necessary arrangements at the first opportunity.

My work has been made easier by the Open University Library, the Bodleian Library, the British Library, and the BBC Written Archives at Caversham. I'm indebted to my generous employer, the Open University, for financial assistance in the preparation of this book for publication.

Numerous friends and colleagues have helped me to think through this book. In particular, I thank Clive Baldwin, Sara Haslam, David Johnson, Anne Laurence, W. R. Owens, Lynda Prescott and Dennis Walder at the Open University. Katie Meade worked tirelessly to clear the rights; Yvette Purdy tolerated my absorption in the book and ensured that I didn't forget about the rest of my working life. I've also received help, hints, encouragement and the odd book from the following: Jacques Berthoud,

Martyn Bond, Mary Bonwick, David Cornell, Peter Golphin, Julian Lethbridge, David McDade, Paul Muldoon, James Nohrnberg, Stephen Regan, Ellen Cronan Rose and Lee Zimmerman. The index was prepared by Isobel Fletcher.

This book is dedicated to my family: my wife, Pat, my stepsons, Chris and Neil Atkins, and my parents Jean and Jonathan Brown, who contributed to the book and my general good humour in a range of contrasting ways; there's no better acknowledgement than MacNeice's own toast: 'This is on me and these are yours'.

Chronology

(Including MacNeice's major publications, works cited in the text and major political events)

1904   Birth of Cecil Day Lewis.

1907   Birth of W. H. Auden.
            Birth of Louis MacNeice.

1909   Birth of Stephen Spender.

1914   Death of MacNeice's mother Lily.
            Outbreak of First World War.

1916   Easter uprising in Dublin for an independent Ireland, leading to a protracted war between Irish nationalists and the British state.

1918   End of First World War.

1921   Treaty agreed which leads to the formation of the Irish Free State; Northern Ireland remains part of Britain.

1926   General Strike in Britain.

1927   Day Lewis edits *Oxford Poetry* with Auden.

1929   MacNeice and Spender edit *Oxford Poetry*; MacNeice, *Blind Fireworks*.

1930   MacNeice marries Giovanna Marie Thérèse Babette Ezra (known as Mary); appointment as assistant lecturer in Classics at the University of Birmingham.

1931   Day Lewis, *From Feathers to Iron*.
            Collapse of Ramsay MacDonald's Labour government; formation of 'national' government by MacDonald and others in alliance with Conservatives. Economic slump and mass unemployment.

1932   MacNeice (writing as 'Louis Malone'), *Roundabout Way* (novel); *New Signatures* anthology (ed. Michael Roberts).

1933   Spender, *Poems*; Day Lewis, *The Magnetic Mountain*; *New*

Country anthology (ed. Roberts).
National Socialists seize power in Germany.

1934   Day Lewis, *A Hope for Poetry*; Spender, *Vienna*.
Viennese Socialist uprising.

1935   MacNeice, *Poems*; Spender, *The Destructive Element*; Day Lewis, *A Time to Dance*; birth of MacNeice's son Daniel.

1936   MacNeice, *The Agamemnon of Aeschylus*; divorce of MacNeice and Mary; appointment to the post of lecturer in Greek at Bedford College, University of London.
Outbreak of Spanish Civil War; German reoccupation of demilitarized Rhineland.

1937   Auden and MacNeice, *Letters from Iceland*; MacNeice, *Out of the Picture*; Spender, *Forward from Liberalism*.

1938   MacNeice, *The Earth Compels*; *I Crossed the Minch*; *Modern Poetry*; *Zoo*; Spender, *Trial of a Judge*; Day Lewis, *Overtures to Death*; Auden (ed.), *The Oxford Book of Light Verse*.
German annexation of Austria; Munich Crisis after German claims on the Sudetenland of Czechoslovakia.

1939   MacNeice, *Autumn Journal*; Spender, *The Still Centre*.
Spanish Civil War ends with victory for Franco's nationalists; German annexation of Czechoslovakia then Poland; outbreak of Second World War.

1940   MacNeice, *The Last Ditch*.

1941   MacNeice, *Collected Poems 1925–1940*; *The Poetry of W. B. Yeats*; *Plant and Phantom*; joins the BBC at first as freelance writer, then as permanent member of staff in the Features Department.

1942   MacNeice marries Antoinette Millicent Hedley Anderson (known as Hedli); death of Bishop John MacNeice.

1943   Birth of MacNeice's daughter Brigid Corinna.

1944   MacNeice, *Springboard*; *Christopher Columbus*.

1945   End of Second World War; election of Atlee's Labour government.

1947   MacNeice, *The Dark Tower and Other Radio Scripts*.

1948   MacNeice, *Holes in the Sky*.

1949   MacNeice, *Collected Poems 1925–1948*.

1951   MacNeice, *Goethe's Faust*; Spender, *World within World*.

1952   MacNeice, *Ten Burnt Offerings*.

1954   MacNeice, *Autumn Sequel*.

1957   MacNeice, *Visitations*.

1961   MacNeice, *Solstices*.

1963   MacNeice, *The Burning Perch*.
         3 September: death of MacNeice.

1964   MacNeice, *The Mad Islands* and *The Administrator*.

1965   MacNeice, *The Strings are False: An Unfinished Autobiography; Varieties of Parable*.

1966   *Collected Poems of Louis MacNeice*, ed. E. R. Dodds.

1968   MacNeice, *One for the Grave: A Modern Morality Play*; appointment of Day Lewis as poet laureate.

1969   MacNeice, *Persons from Porlock and Other Plays for Radio*.

1972   Death of Day Lewis.

1973   Death of Auden.

1995   Death of Spender.

2007   *Collected Poems of Louis MacNeice*, ed. Peter McDonald.

Abbreviations

The following abbreviations have been used when quoting from primary sources. See the Select Bibliography for full details.

MacNeice

CP	*Collected Poems of Louis MacNeice*, ed. Peter McDonald (2007)
CPD	*Collected Poems of Louis MacNeice*, ed. E. R. Dodds (1966; 1979)
DT	*The Dark Tower and Other Radio Scripts* (1947)
HS	*Holes in the Sky* (1948)
ICM	*I Crossed the Minch* (1938)
LI	*Letters from Iceland*, with W. H. Auden (1937)
MP	*Modern Poetry: A Personal Essay* (1938)
Plays	*Selected Plays of Louis MacNeice*, ed. Alan Heuser and Peter McDonald (1993)
Prose	*Selected Prose of Louis MacNeice*, ed. Alan Heuser (1990)
PY	*The Poetry of W. B. Yeats* (1941)
S.	*Springboard: Poems 1941–1944* (1944)
SF	*The Strings are False: An Unfinished Autobiography*, ed. E. R. Dodds (1965)
SLC	*Selected Literary Criticism of Louis MacNeice*, ed. Alan Heuser (1987)
VP	*Varieties of Parable* (1965)

Day Lewis

CPDL	*The Complete Poems of C. Day Lewis* (1992)
HP	*A Hope for Poetry* (1934, 1936)
TD	*A Time to Dance and Other Poems* (1935)

Spender

DE	*The Destructive Element: A Study of Modern Writers and Beliefs* (1935)
NCP	*New Collected Poems*, ed. Michael Brett (2004)
WW	*World within World: the Autobiography of Stephen Spender* (1951)

Introduction: 'Our End is Life'

The first poem by Louis MacNeice I read was 'Thalassa'. I was 14 or 15, studying for my Engl. Lit. O level in the early 1980s; the set text was *The New Dragon Book of Verse*. I already thought that I liked poetry, but the only poet I approved of was Shelley – because of his reputation for atheism and anarchism – and the only actual poems of his I'd read were shorts like 'Dirge' ('Wail, for the world's wrong' was instantly resonant) and 'The Mask of Anarchy', chiefly, I'm afraid, because of the transgressive (but not wholly understood) thrill of its title. I thought the *New Dragon* was a bit of a bore. It had worthy things like Gaunt's Dying Speech, of whose sentiments I disapproved, classics like Gray's *Elegy*, which I quite liked but felt I should resist.[1] 'Thalassa' came in a section with the not altogether enticing title 'Seascapes': it was set alongside things like 'Cargoes' (it would take Paul Muldoon's inspired pastiche of Masefield in the voices of both MacNeice and Auden for me to see any value in 'Quinquireme of Nineveh')[2] and James Elroy Flecker's 'The Old Ships', another poem whose lushness I enjoyed but felt I ought for some reason to discount.

'Thalassa' (*CP* 783) was immediately different. I was by now used to odd-sounding titles, but the oddness didn't continue into the poem:

> Run out the boat, my broken comrades;
> Let the old seaweed crack, the surge
> Burgeon oblivious of the last
> Embarkation of feckless men,
> Let every adverse force converge –
> Here we must needs embark again.

> (*CP*, 783)

1

Again, I was used to poems which sounded beautiful – that is, whose vocabulary and idiom gave the effect of some sort of linguistic intoxication: 'I watched in vain/ To see the mast burst open with the rose,/ And the whole deck put on its leaves again' struck me like this.[3] But what was unusual about 'Thalassa' was that such inflated vocabulary – 'Burgeon oblivious'; 'every adverse force converge' – coexisted with something like conversational English. 'Run out the boat, my broken comrades' sounded like someone talking directly in a language I understood.

Yet the charge the poem held for me was something to do with its tone of exhaustion and enigmatic regret; the way the speaker seemed disabused both of callow optimism and any residual faith in traditional values – the same values, perhaps, I imputed to the rest of the *New Dragon*:

> Run up the sail, my heartsick comrades;
> Let each horizon tilt and lurch –
> You know the worst: your wills are fickle,
> Your values blurred, your hearts impure
> And your past life a ruined church –
> But let your poison be your cure.

This was more like it: this was the kind of emotion I expected of 'poetry'. 'Your values blurred, your hearts impure' sounded precisely like a description of what I felt living in the north of England in the early 1980s was like. The fantastic line, 'And your past life a ruined church' had the kind of rhetorical glamour and social agenda I required. The past is bankrupt, I took the poem to be saying; traditional values, symbolized by religion, are unsustaining and inadequate. Drastic measures are needed: 'let your poison be your cure'; there is an urgent imperative to change your life.

This suggests that I rapidly evolved a very slick, adolescent approach to the poem. At that stage, I had no sense that MacNeice was revisiting Tennyson's 'Ulysses'; though we were told that 'Thalassa' was the Greek for 'the sea', I wasn't very interested in this kind of detail. But the other thing I remember about this first reading is that its imagery perplexed the teacher who was at a loss to explain the final stanza:

2

> Put out to sea, ignoble comrades,
> Whose record shall be noble yet;
> Butting through scarps of moving marble
> The narwhal dares us to be free;
> By a high star our course is set,
> Our end is Life. Put out to sea.

What on earth does 'Butting through scarps of moving marble' mean, she wondered? A ship can't pass through a scarp (that is, she glossed, a steep face) of 'moving marble': it doesn't make any kind of sense. Though I remember disagreeing, I didn't have the vocabulary to suggest that the almost surreal imagery of this stanza was both in keeping with the poem as a whole ('Let every adverse force converge': you can't imagine forces any more adverse than scarps of moving marble, can you?) and that it suited the poem's broader agenda. If your past life and your values are bankrupt, if you are variously broken, feckless, fickle and impure, then you have nothing to fall back on. You have to 'Put out to sea', even if that is a terrifying sea of 'moving marble', because 'Our end is Life'. I liked the capital letter: it embodied what I took to be the poem's existential challenge: you don't have any options in this poisonous world: 'Our end is Life. Put out to sea.' It sounded like a call to arms. Yet it is one which with the passage of time becomes more plausible because of the poem's relentless emphasis on failure, on heartsickness and an absence of courage or worthiness. The tempting paradox which the poem offers is that, although you are 'ignoble', through the business of putting out to sea in inauspicious conditions you have the slim chance of making your record noble, of – against all the odds and your own expectations – amounting to something. 'The narwhal dares us to be free': at 15 this sounded darkly liberating; it still retains that mysterious charge.

I begin with this memory for two reasons. Firstly, because 'Thalassa' remains a good way to begin an acquaintance with MacNeice. Though it is printed in both E. R. Dodds's and Peter McDonald's editions of the *Collected Poems* as MacNeice's final poem, Robyn Marsack has revealed that it may have been drafted in the mid-1940s and considered for inclusion in the *Springboard* volume of 1944.[4] Such ambiguity enhances the poem's resonance. Considered as a final poem, it is, as Marsack observes, 'triumphant': a poem which at once encapsulates a sense of the limitations of human life and yet manages to affirm its values in a way which is both compelling and undeceived.[5] But as a wartime poem, 'Thalassa' becomes more embroiled in the circumstances of its composition. Rather than being an abstract assertion of courage, it can be read as a text which responds to the uncertainties of the early 1940s with a mixture of fatalism and resistant idealism: though 'Your values blurred, your hearts impure', by the close of the poem MacNeice reaffirms that 'By a high star our course is set'. High stars, of course, never guarantee ultimate success, but they do endorse 'the last/ Embarkation of feckless men' as a journey which must be undertaken. Such sentiments, often expressed in a more minor key, are common in *Springboard*, as MacNeice attempted to write a poetry which might convey the bleakness and cost of war alongside the struggle between antithetical value systems which that war embodied. As we shall see, MacNeice's poetry is often poised between its facility with plausible generalization and a sense of subservience to the circumstances in which it was written. Or, as I recognized from that first reading of 'Thalassa', between an impulse to hyperbole ('Let ... the surge/ Burgeon') and a potentially contradictory impulse towards the immediate, the conversational ('Put out to sea'). Such impulses are characteristic both of MacNeice and the literary generation he was a part of.

My second reason for beginning with autobiography is because MacNeice's own criticism foregrounds his experience as a reader as a way of helping to explain to others the value he found in poetry. MacNeice and his contemporaries have often been criticized for their autobiographical tendencies. Arguably, Christopher Isherwood's novels only succeed when they are centred on a central character who either is called 'Christopher Isherwood' or has experiences and an outlook that mirror those of his creator. Similarly, MacNeice, Spender and Day Lewis all wrote autobiographies (though MacNeice's was published posthumously); there are times when their poetry depends on autobiographical and anecdotal detail. And yet for all the sense that these writers were overly reliant on autobiographical materials, at their best their absorption in their own lives makes for texts which have the capacity to make direct contact with the imaginative worlds of their readers. I also want to suggest that the practice of MacNeice and Spender offers a salutary corrective to the more controlled and – arguably – colourless discourses of contemporary academic criticism. Though, in recent years, critics have rightly become sceptical of transhistorical claims to literary excellence and conscious of the political values and assumptions which underpin their work, there is a countervailing risk that we lose a sense of the pleasures of reading which remain shadily at the heart of the practice of literary criticism.

I write 'shadily' because literary pleasure is seldom unalloyed and because any consideration of MacNeice and his contemporaries necessarily involves the critic in twentieth-century history and the ways in which these self-conscious poets responded to the political and intellectual turmoils through which they lived. Writers like MacNeice and Spender didn't write about themselves either because they were just egoists or because they couldn't think of anything better to write about. As *Modern Poetry* demonstrates, MacNeice uses his own experience as a reader as a way of querying T. S. Eliot's claim that there is no connection between the literary tastes of a child and an adult and his broader theory of poetic impersonality. MacNeice's presentation of his reading as a 'case-book' demonstrates the influence of modish psychological theory on his conception of literary history:

> I would contend [...] that the adolescent's reaction to poetry has an identity with the child's reaction, just as, according to modern psychologists, sex-life does not begin at adolescence but at birth. [...] Having during my childhood and adolescence visited both the poles of traditionalism and of free-lance experimentation, I feel that a survey of these journeys and a return from these towards a conception of living tradition (distinguished from dead traditionalism) may illustrate *in parvo* and more simply the interflux of extremist principles in modern poetry which is gradually resolving itself towards that same conception. (*MP* 35)

At one level this is subjective writing ('I would contend'; 'I feel that') of a kind which typically makes would-be objective critics nervous. Yet part of the strength of MacNeice's work lies in the ways in which he makes his own experiences available to the reader as a readily generalizable 'case-book'. This, the reader is persuaded into feeling, is exactly how someone of that

5

background would have reacted to these stimuli; this makes me understand the literary psychology of an upper-middle-class, left-leaning writer of the 1930s. In rereading the poetry of MacNeice and his contemporaries, I suggest that this work retains its relevance precisely because of these generalizing manoeuvres. And I think this is what struck a chord with me when I first read 'Thalassa' in the early 1980s. MacNeice's poem seemed closer to me and to my world of punk rock, the Thatcher government and the usual adolescent angst than did, say, the *Elegy Written in a Country Church-Yard*, or even Auden's 'On This Island' (also present in the *New Dragon*). I'm not saying that 'Thalassa' is directly congruent with or responsive to these very different contexts; nonetheless, it is a poem (like many of MacNeice's best) which continues to resonate because it is pitched in ordinary yet memorable language and tuned to the experience and dilemmas of ordinary people. 'Our end is Life': precisely.

*

This book focuses chiefly on the poetry of Louis MacNeice in the belief that he is one of the major poets of the twentieth century. As my conclusion suggests, he has been a major influence on contemporary poets, especially in Ireland. In spite of this, he remains a less prominent figure than Yeats, Eliot or Auden. Literary histories such as Samuel Hynes's *The Auden Generation* and Valentine Cunningham's *British Writers of the Thirties* present MacNeice as an Audenesque also-ran whose only significant differences from the pack of would-be Wystans were his laconic melancholia, Irishness and lack of political conviction at a time when membership of the Communist Party was a fashionable poetic accessory.[6] Reacting against reductive views, Edna Longley and Peter McDonald have stressed the ways in which he differs from his English contemporaries and the individual quality of his poetic achievement.[7] This has tended to mean, as Terence Brown has recognized, that critics have underestimated 'his political and social commitments' and – in the interests of locating his work more precisely in Irish concerns – have neglected 'the English MacNeice'.[8]

This intellectual context accounts for the structure of this study. Though MacNeice is one of the previous century's most distinctive poets, it is inarguable that he was part of a group of writers, most of whom were educated at public school and Oxford, who published their work in the same periodicals, who lived and worked in London during the 1930s, who mixed in the same social networks, and who shared similar political and aesthetic views. MacNeice collaborated with Auden on *Letters from Iceland* (a collection which includes that most unlikely of literary products, a jointly written poem) while his autobiography concedes his play *Out of the Picture* is an example of his 'mortifying my aesthetic sense by trying to write as Wystan did' (*SF* 169). MacNeice's life or work cannot be extricated from the literary culture of the decade in which he came to prominence. Throughout his career, the works of Auden, Spender and, to a lesser extent, Day Lewis, are sympathetic touchstones through which he assesses poetry. This study is therefore centred on MacNeice, but makes space, especially in chapter 2, for Spender and Day Lewis. I am not, however, wanting to reinscribe an unproblematic idea of 'the Auden generation' or a '1930s group'. As recent criticism has indicated, the connections between these writers are almost as interesting for the deviations and swerves in emphasis between them: there was no single manifesto to which they signed up; their literary and political affiliations were complicated and troubled, and there was no automatic loyalty between different 'members of the group'. MacNeice provides a telling example: reviewing Auden and Isherwood's play *On the Frontier* for the *Spectator* in November 1938, he noted, 'The mystical love scenes of Eric and Anna made one long for a sack to put one's head in' (*SLC* 101).[9] In reading MacNeice alongside his contemporaries, I want not only to restore awareness of 'the English MacNeice' but to investigate the complexity of what might be called literary group dynamics. What was it that bracketed these writers together in the early 1930s; what kept them in contact with one another after the 1930s; and how useful is the idea of a group to understanding their poetry?

A further reason for including Spender and Day Lewis in this study is the hope that it will stimulate renewed interest in their work. Though MacNeice's canonical status is relatively assured, the same cannot be said for Spender and Day Lewis. Ian Hamilton's waspish *Against Oblivion*, a book which aims to select about fifty twentieth-century poets whose work might avoid being forgotten, views Spender as 'thoroughly old-fashioned' and 'muddle-headed', while Day Lewis does not make the cut, being dismissed in the Introduction with the amazed question, 'who, one might even ask, would speak of C. Day Lewis?'[10] Hamilton may turn out to be right: having been poet laureate has never been an insurance against oblivion, and his list of once-celebrated twentieth-century poets already slipping out of view does not include several of MacNeice's contemporaries whose work was widely disseminated in fashionable period-icals.[11] My concern is not so much with whether or not Day Lewis or Spender will be read in the future but with the fact that their work was important both for the literary culture of the 1930s and for MacNeice's own developing poetics: alongside Auden, their work furnishes *Modern Poetry* with key examples of the change in poetic attitude he identifies in its first chapter. These close relations and literary dialogues inflect both MacNeice's life and many of his poems. In this light, the future student of MacNeice and Auden will need more than a passing acquaintance with the poetry of Spender and Day Lewis.

*

MacNeice was a prolific writer; as he recognized, 'my trouble all my life has been *over*-production'.[12] A study of this kind demands selectivity. With a writer as fecund as MacNeice, this demand is all the more pressing. Though little that he wrote is without interest, his oeuvre divides between the poetry and the rest. I make no apology for concentrating on the poetry: it is this body of work which continues to excite new readers and which has been influential on later writers. Because of limited space, my method is to focus on selected poems in detail to give readers a concentrated flavour of MacNeice's work as opposed to a more diffuse survey. His criticism and drama provide contexts for the poetry which are drawn on throughout. My focus raises the question of how to approach the poetry. As I write in early 2007, the centennial publication of Peter McDonald's new edition of the *Collected Poems* has transformed the study of MacNeice. This volume enables readers for the first time for many years to read MacNeice's poetry as it was originally published in volume form. Unlike his predecessor

(MacNeice's literary executor, E. R. Dodds), McDonald critically revises the editorial decisions MacNeice took for *Collected Poems 1925–1948*, which omitted many poems and resequenced the contents of individual volumes. In the process, MacNeice disguised when the texts were first collected and dismantled the often subtle internal architecture of the original volumes.[13] Like McDonald, I privilege these volumes because they show MacNeice working at different moments in time, not just the revising poet in mid-passage of 1949.

1

MacNeice and the
Modern Everyman

MacNEICE AND THE AUTOBIOGRAPHICAL MODE

During the 1960s Auden lamented, 'It is a sad fact [...] that a poet can earn much more money writing or talking about his art than he can by practicing it'.[1] Though this suggests a reluctance to write criticism, the poets of the 1930s were keen to theorize their work especially during that decade. As one commentator quips, 'It almost seems as if the main task of many poets was to make an assertion about the poet's function, rather than to perform that function'.[2] Economics may underlie this eagerness, but the fact remains that the literature of the period provides several 'defences of poetry': MacNeice, Spender and Day Lewis each made their own contributions to the genre. MacNeice's description of his ideal poet, in *Modern Poetry*, has been widely quoted as a shorthand sketch of a 'typical' 1930s poet. It also tells us much about MacNeice himself and his relationship with his contemporaries:

> My own prejudice [...] is in favour of poets whose worlds are not too esoteric. I would have a poet able-bodied, fond of talking, a reader of the newspapers, capable of pity and laughter, informed in economics, appreciative of women, involved in personal relationships, actively interested in politics, susceptible to physical impressions. (*MP* 198)

MacNeice recalls similar statements by Auden. The caution about esoteric poets glances towards the intimidating figure of W. B. Yeats, and echoes Auden's argument, outlined in his Introduction to *The Oxford Book of Light Verse* (1938), that the modern poet should reject post-Romantic ideas of 'pure poetry'

10

in favour of writing which engages directly with the concerns of 'a genuine community'.[3] MacNeice's poet seems to embody this egalitarian fantasy. He is someone palpably plugged into the 'real' world, whose attributes stress a zest for living, alongside intellectual curiosity. Being 'informed in economics' and 'appreciative of women' are equally important to this sociable and empathetic poet.

Though this last phrase may strike twenty-first-century readers as hopelessly dated, with its assumption that 'the poet' *must* be male and the implication that 'he' will be heterosexual, it signals MacNeice's divergence from Audenesque attitudes. 'Appreciative of women' implicitly rebukes Auden, whose early work tended to be hostile especially to mothers. This is apparent in the plays he wrote with the equally misogynistic Isherwood. Michael Ransom's mother in *The Ascent of F6* (1936) is a domineering matriarch whose ambition for her son coincides with her desire to control him. In the words of one of Auden's creepy songs, 'You shall be mine, all mine,/ You shall have kisses like wine,/ When the wine gets into your head/ Mother will see that you're not misled'.[4] MacNeice's mother died when he was 7 after being hospitalized two years earlier. 'Autobiography' connects his own depression to his mother's sudden – and to the child – horribly enigmatic departure:

> My mother wore a yellow dress;
> Gently, gently gentleness.
>
> *Come back early or never come.*
>
> When I was five the black dreams came;
> Nothing after was quite the same.

> (CP 200)

For MacNeice, the rejection of mothers and women in general by his homosexual contemporaries was unconvincing. That dissent from a misogynist consensus is implicit in *Modern Poetry*. Like many other definitions of the role of the poet, MacNeice's is incidentally informative about the writer himself. When *Modern Poetry* was published in November 1938, MacNeice was 31, divorced from his first wife (with whom he had a son), involved in a protracted relationship with the artist Nancy Sharp (who was then married to the painter William Coldstream and would later marry Spender's elder brother Michael), employed as a lecturer in Greek at Bedford College while simultaneously working on numerous literary projects. In 1938 he published his third collection of poetry, *The Earth Compels*, two prose works unashamedly written for the money (*I Crossed the Minch* and *Zoo*), as well as several book reviews and poems in periodicals. During the second half of that year, he drafted *Autumn Journal*, arguably the major long poem of the period, which reflects on contemporary events, particularly the imminent possibility of another war between Britain and Germany, and which would be published in the spring of 1939. Whether or not this schedule left much time for reading newspapers, it probably demanded an 'able-bodied' constitution.

As I have suggested, MacNeice deployed autobiographical techniques as a means of making contact between his experiences and those of his readers. MacNeice's concern with his own life, moreover, connects with fundamental poetic tenets to which he remained faithful throughout his career. Though *Modern Poetry* centres on MacNeice as an individual, it also reacts against older definitions of the poet. His conception of the poet as 'a specialist in something which every one practises' and as 'a blend of the entertainer and the critic or informer' (*MP* 31, 197) dissents from both the Romantic model (deriving from Shelley) of the poet as an 'unacknowledged legislator' and T. S. Eliot's view that twentieth-century poets should make their work complex and allusive.[5] MacNeice's poet is neither a misunderstood outsider nor a 'difficult' Modernist, but is a specialized entertainer. Like Auden, and like most of his generation, MacNeice wanted to revise the public perception of the poet. But unlike Auden, MacNeice did not fundamentally change his mind about these issues after the 1930s. In his final book of criticism, *Varieties of Parable*, MacNeice returns to a formulation he admired from Christopher Caudwell's Marxist literary history, *Illusion and Reality*:

> Caudwell, who rightly insisted that poetry was by its nature subjective, went on to describe it as the medium through which man retires into his inner self, *thereby to regain communion with his fellows*. (*VP* 27–8)[6]

Caudwell's theory accounts for the autobiographical mode of much of MacNeice's writing. Though it would be misleading to describe MacNeice's life as 'ordinary', he repeatedly insists on the richness of ordinary experience and uses his own life as an example of the everyday; as *Autumn Sequel* puts it, 'Everydayness is good' (*CP* 397). This sort of poet is not simply a purveyor of the mundane, but is a man, as MacNeice himself was, embroiled in – crucially, not bored by – the business of the everyday life and social interaction. If the Shelleyan poet is an outsider who lives beyond social mores, the MacNeicean poet is a figure who, while remaining sceptical about convention and authority, works within, and defines his identity against, large institutions. Because it is this everyday life which MacNeice makes the centre of his work, and because it is through this fabric of the quotidian that he strives 'to regain communion with his fellows', we need to explore his life in more detail.

NOTES FOR A BIOGRAPHY

The late poem 'Notes for a Biography' evokes 'An oranges (sweet) and lemons (bitter) childhood' (*CP* 529). Though not autobiographical, the poem articulates MacNeice's recurrent preoccupation with the ambiguities of childhood. It is a period dominated by 'Voices of duty or magic' alongside 'the double/ Feeling that all is new and that all has happened before'. In *Blind Fireworks*, his first volume, 'Child's Unhappiness' evokes a 'memoried distress' as the speaker tries to understand his 'tortured self' (*CP* 618). The final volume, *The Burning Perch*, includes 'Children's Games', a breathless, criss-cross sampler of lines from games and nursery rhymes which manages to be both nostalgic and unsettling in its knowing metaphoric appropriation of familiar phrases: 'I'm the king of the barbican, come down you dirty charlatan./ When you see a magpie put salt upon her tail' (*CP* 594).

Yet his images of childhood are not in one key only. 'The Cyclist' captures the joy of summer cycling: 'In the heat of the handlebars he grasps the summer'; 'When We Were Children' juxtaposes the complexity of adult emotion with the more spontaneous responses of a past when 'Spring was easy,/ Dousing our heads in suds of hawthorn/ And scrambling the laburnum tree' (*CP* 270, 250). Because MacNeice remained in

13

touch with these traumas and joys – and most importantly the physical impressions which they made on him – his poetry is sensitive to the overlaps between adult experience and childhood. These connections frequently threaten to become discontinuous and enigmatic. The first section of 'Notes for a Biography' concludes:

> Call it despair or delight
> (Or both), it went. The ringers in St Clement's
> Rang their bells down and under the arch of hands
> He escaped, or was carried away, from those ups and downs of
>   childhood.

MacNeice returns to the nursery rhyme used in the first line to capture 'the double/ Feeling' of childhood. The game connected with 'Oranges and Lemons' stages the mock execution of one of the players who is caught 'under the arch of hands'.[7] At one level, the poem's protagonist 'escaped, or was carried away' from the game, yet the phrase gains a broader metaphoric resonance which raises the question of how any of us grow up: is it a process of escape or abduction? And was your childhood characterized by 'despair or delight', 'Or' – more probably – 'both'?

MacNeice was the third child of the Reverend John MacNeice and Lily Clesham.[8] Both families were from Connemara in the west of Ireland. John MacNeice's career as a Church of Ireland minister took his young family first to Belfast, where Louis was born, and later to Carrickfergus. John would go on to become Bishop of Cashel and Waterford in 1931 and Bishop of Down, Connor and Dromore in 1934. The MacNeice family felt troubled and isolated in the north. Louis's elder brother Willie was a slow learner and was subsequently diagnosed as a Down's syndrome child, a condition then labelled as mongolism. Lily believed that Willie's apparent backwardness was in some way her fault. In the years after Louis's birth she became increasingly depressed, partly also because she had not settled in the north and hankered to return to the west. After a hysterectomy for a uterine fibroid (which both Lily and Louis erroneously believed was caused by giving birth to him) she retreated into a nursing home, dying at the age of 48 in 1914.

According to *The Strings are False*, MacNeice's childhood was dominated by a sense of isolation. He was terrified of his father, who seemed to him distant and inscrutable, involved in a 'conspiracy with God', and by the threat of hell instilled into him by a 'Mother's Help' (*SF* 38, 41). His isolation was exacerbated by a lack of contact with local children: MacNeice was educated at home and saw little of the town of Carrickfergus. He had a keen sense of his ambivalent social position:

> The Lower Classes were dour and hostile, they would never believe what you said. Not that the Gentry were much better; even then I was conscious that to be the son of a clergyman was to be something the Gentry only half accepted and that in a patronising way. (*SF* 58)

Though MacNeice dramatizes with the benefit of hindsight, his early childhood seems to have been genuinely remote from the rest of Northern Irish society and rich in the kinds of imaginative experience used in his poems. 'Voices of duty or magic', and the incipient sense of the conflict between these voices, shaped his horizons.

After his father's remarriage in 1917, MacNeice was sent to school in England. He went to Sherborne prep school, where he was taught by the charismatic headmaster Littleton Powys, brother of the novelists John Cowper, Llewelyn and T. F. Powys. Though their paths did not cross, Day Lewis attended the senior school at this time. From Sherborne, MacNeice moved to Marlborough College, where fellow pupils included the future art historian and Soviet spy Anthony Blunt (with whom MacNeice formed a close friendship) and the poet John Betjeman (with whom he did not). Louis's Irishness marked him out as being different. The contrast between England and Ireland is central to 'Carrickfergus' (*CP* 55–6), in which MacNeice juxtaposes the 'camp of soldiers' he saw in Northern Ireland after the outbreak of the First World War 'with long/ Dummies hanging from gibbets for bayonet practice' with the tamer world of Sherborne:

> I went to school in Dorset, the world of parents
> Contracted into a puppet world of sons
> Far from the mill girls, the smell of porter, the salt-mines,
> And the soldiers with their guns.

> (*CP* 55–6)

Though this suggests an almost magisterial detachment from this 'puppet world', MacNeice was a social and academic success at Sherborne and Marlborough, eventually getting a scholarship to read Classics at Merton College, Oxford.

In addition to the intellectual training MacNeice received at public school, this period is important because it gave him an abiding sense of how people behave in institutions. As 'Carrickfergus' implies, MacNeice quickly appreciated that Sherborne was a radically different milieu from his home, where shifting rules demanded new modes of behaviour. *The Strings are False* reflects in detail on the institutional lessons MacNeice learned at school. On his first arrival at Sherborne,

> The matron [...] told us we must not talk and at last we were left alone. The two little boys began to talk at once. This astonished me. I had been disobedient in my time but not in this way, not as a matter of course. When disobeying Miss Craig I had felt enormous guilt. That the two little boys should disobey so promptly, easily, even automatically, was disconcerting, contrary to nature. It was my first and greatest shock in an English school. To obey one's elders ceased to be an axiom. (*SF* 64)

This decoupling of disobedience from guilt and the concomitant scepticism it induces anticipates MacNeice's rejection of his father's religion. The sense of the arbitrary nature of institutional behaviour is at its most intense in the description of a 'basketing' at Marlborough:

> Once in a while [...] Big Fire [an oligarchy of Upper School boys] decided that someone was undesirable and could therefore provide a Roman Holiday. They would seize him, tear off most of his clothes and cover him with house-paint, then put him in the basket and push him round and round the hall. Meanwhile Little Fire [the mass of Lower School boys], dutifully sitting at their desks, would howl with delight – a perfect exhibition of mass sadism. The masters considered this a fine old tradition, and any boy who had been basketed was under a cloud for the future. Because the boys have an innate sense of justice, anyone they basket must be really undesirable. Government of the mob, by the mob, and for the mob. (*SF* 84–5)

Auden remarked in the early 1930s, 'The best reason I have for opposing Fascism is that at school I lived in a Fascist state'; MacNeice's account is both more temperate and more searching.[9] 'Government by the mob' is disturbing enough, but it is the bland collusion of the masters in this 'fine old tradition' which exposes Marlborough's disciplinary structures as brutal and arbitrary. MacNeice presents himself in *The Strings are False* as a survivor, a non-sporty boy who adapted himself to this potentially fatal flaw by positioning himself as a wit. Tacitly, the basketing episode points to how vital it is to find means of surviving in such an environment. An earlier account in *I Crossed the Minch* focuses on MacNeice's reactions by transposing the anecdote into the voice of Perceval, a laconic alter ego:

> This night the howling was worse than usual and MacNeice, astonished by its crescendo, turned in his desk at the top end of the room. [...] In the basket sat a boy who had been beaten up and had most of his clothes torn off him. His face and neck were thickly covered with red and blue paint, so that he looked liked [*sic*] a carnival figure until you noticed the misery of his eyes. (*ICM* 89)

As MacNeice notices 'the misery of his eyes', observer mirrors victim. Though Perceval notes that the 'mild sadism' of Marlborough 'appealed' to MacNeice, the basketing stands in both *The Strings are False* and *I Crossed the Minch* as a symbol of institutionalized 'barbarity' (*ICM* 88).

MacNeice was academically successful at Oxford, getting a First in his finals much to the surprise of his tutor. His accounts of this time are shot through with a sense of the limitations of the Ivory Tower. Though he concedes 'If it were not for Lit. Hum. I might be climbing/ A ladder with a hod' (an unlikely career move even for someone who wasn't 'real' gentry), *Autumn Journal* explains the intellectual pleasures MacNeice derived from studying Greats – 'it really was very attractive to be able to talk about tables/ And to ask if the table *is*' – alongside a critique of the abstraction of Philosophy at Oxford:

> And they said 'The man in the street is so naïve, he never
> > Can see the wood for the trees;
> He thinks he knows he sees a thing but cannot
> > Tell you how he knows the thing he thinks he sees.'
> And oh how much I liked the Concrete Universal,
> > I never thought that I should
> Be telling them vice-versa
> > That they can't see the trees for the wood.

> (*CP* 130–1)

Autumn Journal is very much a poem of its time. From the perspective of 1938, MacNeice diagnoses that the Oxford of the 1920s did not get to grips with 'the perennial if unimportant problem/ Of getting enough to eat'. At the time he was an undergraduate, MacNeice was much less socially conscious, positioning himself as a heterosexual aesthete in an Oxford divided between homosexual intellectuals and heterosexual hearties (*SF* 103). *Blind Fireworks*, published while he was still an undergraduate, shows little evidence of social awareness. These often intriguing poems focus on childhood, while exhibiting a pervasive debt to T. S. Eliot. Yet the doubleness of MacNeice's later perspective on Oxford is in keeping with his ambiguity about school and the other institutions he was a part of. In a beautifully deft piece of mockery, *Autumn Journal*'s account of Oxford ends with lines which simultaneously repudiate and elegize the university and its values:

> Good-bye now, Plato and Hegel,
> The shop is closing down;
> They don't want any philosopher-kings in England,
> There ain't no universals in this man's town.

> (*CP* 132)

Vocabulary and idiom shift from line to line. The unrhymed lines wistfully and with a suggestion of neoclassical decorum bid farewell to Oxford at a time when England no longer appreciated its singularity; the rhymed lines mischievously veer into the demotic ('There ain't no [...]') and rebrand the university as a shop. Which, in essence, it is, and which would indeed have partially to close during the Second World War. It takes a writer of MacNeice's alertness to institutional psychology and historical process to make this critique.

After Oxford and his marriage in 1930 to Mary Ezra (the stepdaughter of a don) MacNeice got the post of lecturer in Classics at the University of Birmingham. His mentor was E. R. Dodds, a distinguished classicist who would eventually become his literary executor. For the first time in his life, MacNeice was outside of the predominantly upper-middle-class milieux of public school and Oxford. This was a culture shock for the still snobbish young man:

18

I entered Josiah Mason's foundation without realising that it was as different from Oxford as Josiah was from Walter de Merton. [...] [The students] were all so unresponsive, so undernourished, I just could not be bothered. My snobbery was by this stage willing to accept a clean-cut working-man but it could not accept these hybrids. Many of them came from working-class homes but they were all set on finding a berth in the lower middle or the middle middle classes. (SF 131)

Though MacNeice writes as though wanting to become middle class was the most reprehensible ambition imaginable (he goes onto lament 'an alarming proportion were preparing to be school-teachers') his work in Birmingham eventually made him more conscious of different kinds of social experience. In the early 1930s, Auden and Day Lewis remained in the largely congenial ghetto of the prep school; Spender had independent means, which enabled him to spend most of the decade travelling.

This is not simply to suggest that MacNeice had a richer sense of class than his contemporaries. The point is rather that his political ambivalence and his awareness of his own social position contribute to the complex mixture of empathy, aggression and self-scrutiny in his work. Early on in *Autumn Journal*, MacNeice explores the predicament of ordinary people at the end of the August bank holiday. The text refuses to settle for a single attitude towards its subject. On the one hand, it castigates those returning to 'the eight-hour day' as conformists: 'Most are accepters, born and bred to harness,/ And take things as they come' (CP 105–6). On the other hand, it canvasses the possibility of revolutionary change: 'But some refusing harness and more who are refused it/ Would pray that another and a better Kingdom come'. Even here, MacNeice hedges his bets: revolutionary feeling is 'travestied in slogans' as graffiti, though the status quo is then attacked as 'an utterly lost and daft/ System that gives a few at fancy prices/ Their fancy lives'. The brilliance of this passage lies in its dramatization of MacNeice's hesitations and evasions. While he largely endorses a Socialist critique of capitalism, he does not sentimentalize the working classes or revolutionary politics, nor does he attempt to disguise his own social prejudices. He has 'the slave-owner's mind' himself and languorously envisages snapping his fingers to 'find/ Servants or houris ready to wince and flatter/ And build with their degradation your self-esteem'. The critique of the 'lost and daft/ System' works because MacNeice exposes his contradictory social impulses: he neither elevates his conscience nor preaches conventionally. In contrast, Day Lewis's lyric 'Oh hush thee, my baby', from the long poem 'A Time to Dance' apostrophizes the child of slum dwellers in a sentimental, almost Dickensian, indictment of capitalism. Day Lewis's ventriloquizing of working-class idioms is awkward, and the poem reads as something written to prove that he was thinking the 'right' thoughts: 'Thy mother is crying,/ Thy dad's on the dole:/ Two shillings a week is/ The price of a soul' (*TD* 55).[10]

MacNeice's marriage broke down in 1935 shortly after the birth of his son Daniel. He moved to the University of London in 1936 to lecture at Bedford College. As I have mentioned, in the years leading up to the outbreak of the Second World War, MacNeice published widely. As well as the works of 1938 and 1939, he produced the novel *Roundabout Way* (1932) (under the pseudonym Louis Malone), *Poems* (1935), *The Agamemnon of Aeschylus* (1936), *Out of the Picture* (1937) (both of these plays were performed by the Group Theatre) and, with Auden, *Letters from Iceland* (1937). In the first years of the war, *The Last Ditch* (1940), *Plant and Phantom* (1941) and the American only *Collected Poems 1925–1940* (1940) gathered new poems alongside texts written in the later 1930s. His personal life remained unsettled. He considered emigrating as Auden and Isherwood had done, spending most of 1940 in America. This was partly because of his on-off affair with the American writer Eleanor Clark. But MacNeice had misgivings about the war, or at least how it should influence his behaviour. Unlike Auden and Isherwood, MacNeice's position was complicated by his Irishness. Though he staunchly defended his friends in print on his return to Britain,[11] even before his departure to America MacNeice had decided that he could not run 'away from the War', the accusation which was widely levelled at Auden and Isherwood during 1940 (*CP* 683):

> For five months I had been tormented by the ethical problems of the war. In Ireland most people said to me 'What is it to you?' while many of my friends in England took the line that it was just power politics. Why Poland of all places? And then there was India. I had

decided, however, that any choice was now a choice of evils and that it was clear which was the lesser. [...] I felt that I was not justified in supporting the war verbally unless I were prepared to suffer from it in the way that the unprivileged must suffer. (*SF* 21)

MacNeice demurs both from Irish neutrality and the left-wing consensus that the war was another example of 'power politics' analogous to the Imperial occupation of India. In his view, the threat posed by fascism imposed ethical obligations which he could not avoid. The essay 'Traveller's Return' goes to some length to argue that his return was not ethically motivated, but it reads more as a sophistry which enabled him to avoid joining in the pillory of his emigrant friends (*Prose*, 91). *The Strings are False* – unpublished at this time – with its more nuanced sense that 'any choice was now a choice of evils' carries greater conviction. MacNeice's sense that he should 'suffer... in the way the unprivileged must suffer' informs his subsequent actions and poems. He reported on the Blitz; the poems of *Springboard* (1944) capture the human cost of the bombing alongside the exhilaration of wartime London.

In 1941, MacNeice joined the BBC to work initially on propaganda features.[12] The BBC was to become the most important institution in his life. Though by the 1960s he had gone freelance, his premature death was occasioned by catching pneumonia while recording sound effects for his play *Persons from Porlock*. The impact of MacNeice's work for the BBC on his poetry continues to stimulate debate. For Jon Stallworthy, in the mid-1940s, 'the scriptwriter's work for the BBC upset the natural balance of the poet's perceptions'.[13] Indubitably, MacNeice's association with the BBC affected his literary output. He became a prolific writer of radio plays, several of which were published: *Christopher Columbus* (1944), *The Dark Tower and Other Radio Scripts* (1947), *Goethe's Faust* (1951), as well as posthumous collections.[14] But Stallworthy's suggestion is that features writing was a detrimental influence on the poetry, leading MacNeice away from the writing of taut lyrics to longer, baggier poetic structures. *Springboard*, *Holes in the Sky* (1948), and the final section of *Collected Poems 1925–1948* (1949) include longer poems; *Ten Burnt Offerings* (1952) is a collection of linked, sequential poems in the style of Eliot's *Four Quartets*, while *Autumn Sequel* (1954) is a poem of some 160 pages written in

Dantesque *terza rima* and cantos. The difficulty of establishing a causal connection between working for the BBC and poetic deterioration, however, rests on the fact that MacNeice's interest in longer poems predates his job. 'Poetry To-day' (1935) predicts that 'poets in the near future [will] write longer works [...] which will, for the intelligent reader, supersede the stale and plethoric novel' (*SLC* 42); *Autumn Sequel*, indeed, self-consciously revisits *Autumn Journal*. The BBC provided MacNeice with an institutional niche. The relationship between this institution and his work as a poet was at once delicate, frictive and unpredictable.

During the 1940s, the Features Department was a creative milieu which stimulated MacNeice to experiment with new modes of writing. His interest in parable as a literary mode largely stems from his work as a radio dramatist. His job involved him in collaborations with a wide range of people. Laurence Olivier, Marius Goring, Richard Burton, Margaret Rawlings acted in his plays; William Walton and Benjamin Britten provided scores for them; Dylan Thomas and W. R. Rodgers worked with him in the Features Department. MacNeice's immediate superiors and colleagues were themselves creative individuals who valued his work. MacNeice enjoyed close working relationships with Laurence Gilliam, Francis Dillon and others, all of whom were committed to the possibilities of the new medium.[15] Though the BBC changed MacNeice's poetry, it also afforded him creative latitude and financial security.

His personal life also became more stable during the 1940s. He married the singer Hedli Anderson in 1941; their daughter Brigid Corinna was born in 1943. In the post-war years, MacNeice and his family spent a year in Greece where he worked as director of the British Institute in Athens. His work took him on a number of foreign trips, notably to India, where he reported on the end of the British Raj. The trip stimulated several important poems, including 'Letter from India' (which reflects on events MacNeice had witnessed) and 'Didymus' (a mythopoeic exploration of cultural exchanges between the East and the West). Despite his intermittent frustration with the BBC, it is clear that his job enabled MacNeice to pursue his own interests.

During the 1950s and 1960s, the BBC became a larger and more restrictive organization, less indulgent of maverick poets on its staff. After an unenthusiastic MacNeice was sent on a six-month television training course, he wrote the stage play *One for the Grave* (*c.*1958–60), a savage satire on television, in which the morality play *Everyman* is recast as a game show. In one anecdote about his later years in the Corporation, MacNeice is interrogated by management consultants who want to know what he has been doing during six months of apparent inactivity. Grimly revisiting his role as the school wit, he replied 'Thinking'.[16] The tensions between the individual employee and an increasingly bureaucratic working world surface in 'The Suicide' (*CP* 579). It explores, through the description of his office, the death of an employee who has jumped from a window:

> There are the bills
> In the intray, the ash in the ashtray, the grey memoranda stacked
> Against him, the serried ranks of the box-files, the packed
> Jury of his unanswered correspondence

In spite of the bleakness of its subject, 'The Suicide' contrasts the accumulating, unsympathetic detail of bureaucratic life with the creative energy of the suicidal leap 'By catdrop sleight-of-foot or simple vanishing act'. Through his suicide, 'This man with the shy smile has left behind/ Something that was intact'. A section of *Autumn Sequel* advances the paradox that 'life can be confirmed even in suicide' (*CP* 406): this poem supports that assertion through its recalibration of suicide as a creative act. Like *One for the Grave*, 'The Suicide' is a product of MacNeice's increasing exhaustion with 'grey memoranda stacked/ Against him'. Yet it recognizes that the tension between the individual and institutional structures is unavoidable: the individual can no longer stand alone, if indeed he ever could. MacNeice's protagonist is a modern Everyman, whose consciousness of the shortfall between official responsibility and hidden motivation produces this isolated tragedy.

This sensitivity to paradox, distortion and nightmare under-lying the fabric of ordinary living is characteristic of the poems in the final three volumes, *Visitations* (1957), *Solstices* (1961) and *The Burning Perch* (1963). Just before his death, MacNeice

23

commented that he 'was taken aback by the high proportion of sombre pieces' in *The Burning Perch*, though he goes on to suggest that 'even in the most evil picture the good things, like the sea in one of these poems, are still there round the corner' (*CP* 795–6). Unsurprisingly, this conflict between contradictory impulses in the work reflects similar tensions in the life. MacNeice's marriage broke down in the early 1960s; he then set up house with the actress Mary Wimbush. He became increasingly dependent on alcohol (it is possible that the antibiotics he was given during his final illness failed because of the amount of alcohol in his system). And though his freelance contract with the BBC gave him greater autonomy, it also meant that his financial resources were severely stretched.

Yet it would be misleading to characterize the later MacNeice as a sombre poet. 'Notes for a Biography' is again a good example of the unsettled equilibrium of the later work. The biographical subject is a colonial administrator who struggles with the implications of both decolonization and nuclear war (*CP* 530–1). In the contexts of political upheaval and personal loss, he recognizes his guilt but sees that no court is interested in his confession: 'I too would plead guilty – but where can I plead?' He is an everyman of the colonial elite, registering the experience of twentieth-century history as a process through which he becomes 'Outnumbered, outmoded' and left with the weak hope that 'Common sense, if not love, will still carry the day'. The last section returns to the language of nursery rhyme, echoing 'Lavender's blue': 'Lavender blue for love, lavender green for youth –/ Never is time to retire' (*CP* 531–2).[17] The nursery refrain juxtaposes youth with age, as the speaker attempts to come to terms with the passage of time. The poem is sombre inasmuch as it does not flinch from the effects of age any more than it does from those of global change. Yet the speaker remains responsive 'to the blue and the green in the cry' as he hears the nursery rhyme again, and refuses to surrender to 'whatever/ Doubts may rise from below or terror brood from above'. MacNeice does not deny the reality of doubts and terrors but maintains, like his protagonist, a disabused faith in the value of making 'one gesture before I go'.

SPENDER, DAY LEWIS AND THE IDEA OF THE GROUP

The previous sections have argued that MacNeice used autobiographical materials as a means of making contact with his readers. His poetry attempts, following Caudwell's work, to establish some form of secular communion between the poetic text and its readers. Spender and Day Lewis also relied heavily on autobiography, but for different reasons. If MacNeice's poetic project was to encourage 'a return [...] towards a conception of living tradition (distinguished from dead traditionalism)', he remained resistant to any unproblematic restatement of the Romantic ideal of the poet (*MP* 35). For Spender and Day Lewis, this is much less true. This section considers the cultural, educational and literary connections between the three writers and interrogates the idea that they formed an homogenous literary group.

The family backgrounds and educational experiences of the three poets were directly congruent.[18] Each of their mothers died while they were still children. MacNeice and Day Lewis's fathers were clergymen. All of them were brought up as Protestants, a faith they would abandon as students. All three went to boarding school and Oxford. As undergraduates, they edited *Oxford Poetry*: Day Lewis collaborated with Auden on the 1927 edition; MacNeice and Spender performed the same job in 1929. Day Lewis provides a summary of what they and Auden shared:

> We had all been at public schools: we were schoolboys during the first World War, suffering, though remotely, its stresses. We were all [...] emotionally immature for our years, unsophisticated, vaguely dissatisfied, sure of almost nothing but the vocation we felt for writing poetry.[19]

Though Day Lewis's summary is compelling, he omits the fact that they were not strictly contemporaries. As the eldest, born in 1904, he went to Oxford in 1923; Auden and MacNeice, both born in 1907, went in 1925 and 1926 respectively; Spender – the youngest, born in 1909 – went in 1927. Though all of them knew Auden, they did not meet as a group: as Day Lewis later observed, 'We did not know we were a Movement until the critics told us we were' during the 1930s.[20] MacNeice and Day

Lewis seem to have had little to do with one another. Spender and Day Lewis became friends during the 1930s, especially while they were both Communist Party members. MacNeice and Spender were friends of a kind, but their subsequent accounts of each other are arch and bitchy rather than collegial. In *The Strings are False*, the undergraduate Spender is portrayed as 'the nearest to the popular romantic conception of a poet – a towering angel not quite sure if he was fallen, thinking of himself as the poet always, moving in his own limelight' (*SF* 113).[21] Spender's autobiography, *World within World* (1951) virtually ignores MacNeice. One of the problems with the group is that its membership and internal affiliations were always unclear. Day Lewis's sense of what united the four is attractive because of its lively sense of historical and educational context and its emphasis on the importance of poetic 'vocation'. Yet texts like Isherwood's *Lions and Shadows* (1937) and *Christopher and his Kind* (1976) demonstrate that this poetic emphasis conceals an overlapping clique of largely homosexual writers which centred on Auden, Isherwood and Spender. Though Spender was to change his sexual allegiance, during the early 1930s he was predominantly homosexual. Differences of sexual orientation may underwrite the frictive collegiality of Spender and MacNeice.

Nevertheless, Spender's many recapitulations of his meeting with Auden are crucial to an understanding of the dynamics of this idea – or rather fantasy – of a literary group. Spender stresses his willingness to be guided, instructed and shaped by a more powerful personality:

> Once I told [Auden] I wondered whether I ought to write prose, and he answered: 'You must write nothing but poetry, we do not want to lose you for poetry.' This remark produced in me a choking moment of hope mingled with despair, in which I cried: 'But do you really think I am any good?' 'Of course,' he replied frigidly. 'But why?' 'Because you are so infinitely capable of being humiliated. Art is born of humiliation,' he added in his icy voice – and left me wondering when *he* could feel humiliated. (*WW* 52)

Spender was obsessed with the idea of being a poet, and found in Auden's 'frigid' appreciation confirmation of that ambition. As this passage makes clear, Auden's approval is also implicitly a welcome into his club: '*we* do not want to lose you for poetry'.[22]

Much of its comedy derives from the juxtaposition of Auden's 'icy' intellectualism – the man on the inside with a clear literary programme – with Spender's emotionalism – the unfocused acolyte desperate for an entrée to the group.

Though written years after the events it describes, *World within World* encapsulates the myth of the group, positioning Auden as a precocious cultural tactician, who identifies friends like Isherwood as The Novelist and Day Lewis as a colleague: 'A group of emergent artists existed in his mind, like a cabinet in the mind of a party leader' (*WW* 51–2). The use of a political metaphor is interesting, especially since at this time, none of these writers had moved far from the political values of their parents. The unpublished novel 'Instead of Death' (drafted in 1928) contrasts the soft humanism of Spender's alter ego, Benjamin Saschen, 'who believed in improving humanity and mitigating evil conditions', with the apolitical position advocated by the Auden figure, Vernon Hunter: 'one mustn't fall for a one-sided view of life, a view that says the capitalists are wicked, or that poverty is intolerable, even if, in fact one fights capitalism and poverty. [...] We are the witnesses of the vitality of what is'.[23]

Witnesses or not, as their poems got into print and they started to be identified as a group, politics became important for all four writers. It was the perception that their political ideology was interchangeable which animated the bile of the right-wing poet Roy Campbell, who was later to lampoon them as 'joint MacSpaunday', a cowardly, careerist, charlatan.[24] This has remained part of the literary historical shorthand which defines the 'poets of the 1930s', yet it disguises significant differences between individual poets. Though all four were, like the majority of their contemporaries, profoundly influenced by the collapse of Ramsay MacDonald's Labour government and the formation of a 'national' government in 1931, there was no party line or agreement between them. Day Lewis joined the Communist Party in 1936, leaving it in 1938. Spender joined briefly in 1937, when the Left Book Club published his *Forward from Liberalism*, which tentatively promises to draw 'the outlines of a personal attitude towards communism'.[25] For both writers, the failed hopes of the Spanish Civil War led to a reassessment of their attitudes towards communism and a drift back towards liberalism. Though Auden wrote the curiously opaque poem 'A Communist to Others' in 1932, he never joined the party, despite maintaining left-leaning sympathies throughout his life.[26] MacNeice was the least doctrinaire of the four. *Poems* includes texts such as 'To a Communist' and 'Wolves', which mischievously undermine utopian aspirations: 'Join hands, and make believe that joined/ Hands will keep away the wolves of water/ Who howl along our coast' (*CP* 27).

Yet it would be equally misleading to suggest that they had no political ideas in common. The impulse to revise his past made Auden seem a more apolitical writer than he did during the 1930s. His practice of rewriting and suppressing poems in the light of his changing beliefs depoliticized his canon during his lifetime. Similarly, though Spender and Day Lewis were Communist Party members for brief periods of time, their early poems are politically forthright. Spender's 'The Funeral' gleefully anticipates 'the world state/ With its towns like brain-centres and its pulsing arteries' and mocks 'the crocodile tears of European genius' (*NCP* 18–19). Day Lewis's *A Time to Dance* contains the much derided poem 'Yes, why do we all, seeing a Red, feel small?' which urges that its communist subject 'is what your sons could be, the road these times should take' (*TD* 58–9). Significantly, both poets revised their poetic pasts in the manner of Auden. Along with many of his more politically exuberant early poems, Spender excluded 'The Funeral' from *Collected Poems 1928–1985*. Day Lewis, though not as prone to revision as his colleagues, rewrote *A Time to Dance* to excise the offending poem.

The sense that these poets were following a shared agenda is prominent in Michael Roberts's two anthologies, *New Signatures* (1932) and *New Country* (1933). *New Signatures* included recent poems by Auden, Day Lewis and Spender; *New Country* offered more poems by the same writers alongside prose by Isherwood and Edward Upward among others. For Roberts, all three poets exhibit a reaction 'against esoteric poetry' and solve the problem of how 'to use the material presented by modern civilisation', especially through their use of consciously 'modern' imagery of railways and pylons.[27] Roberts anticipates the wave of critical writings by the poets themselves: Day Lewis's *A Hope for Poetry* (1934), Spender's *The Destructive Element* (1935), and MacNeice's

Modern Poetry, as well as the prominence which their work was to have in Geoffrey Grigson's *New Verse* periodical (1933–9).

And yet there are significant disjunctions even within this wave of group self-publicity. MacNeice is not included in Roberts's anthologies and scarcely figures in the first edition of *A Hope for Poetry*. In a letter to Grigson, Day Lewis asked 'if you could let me know how to come by some of MacNeice's poems. I'd like to say something about him in my book, if he fits in, but I don't want to base criticism on that first book of his'.[28] When Day Lewis got his hands on MacNeice's *Poems*, he was able to comment on it in the Postscript to the 1936 edition of *A Hope for Poetry*. He saw MacNeice as reacting against the *New Signatures*-esque trend he had identified in the body of his text:

> This element is a reaction from the recent preoccupation of poets with social justice, their possibly over-mechanized vocabulary, and often slapdash technique: a return to the ideals of poetic integrity and artistic individualism: a setting-out-again in the direction of 'pure' poetry. Because it expresses this reaction with clarity and conviction, I have referred to MacNeice's 'Poems' as in some ways the most interesting of the poetical work produced in the last two years. (*HP* 80)

Day Lewis's view has been influential on subsequent MacNeice scholarship: it substantially informs Hynes's reading of MacNeice as a melancholy aesthete. Yet as McDonald has observed, it does not sit well with *Modern Poetry*'s 'plea for *impure* poetry' (*MP* v),[29] nor is it a wholly convincing account of the contents of *Poems*. While MacNeice demurs from the language of political solidarity in individual poems, this does not mean that his work can be represented as an unproblematic return to 'artistic individualism'. As the next chapter will argue, MacNeice's 1930s poetry is more socially engaged and more devious than Day Lewis allows for.

So how important is the idea of the literary group to the work of these poets? The links between the three in terms of class background and education are undeniable. Though they never physically constituted themselves as a group, they were aware of one another from the late 1920s. All three admired Auden: he is the major contemporary figure in *A Hope for Poetry*, *The Destructive Element* and *Modern Poetry*. These texts show a pervasive concern with one another's work: the new poetry of *Modern Poetry* is chiefly that of Auden, Spender, and, to a lesser extent, Day Lewis; similarly, *A Hope for Poetry* praises Auden, Spender, and, to a lesser extent, MacNeice.

Such mutual admiration implies that the idea of the group remains important for the understanding of the poetry. Yet there are significant caveats to make. Firstly, as was mentioned in the Introduction, the three did not refrain from attacking one another's work in print. In 1935, MacNeice lambasted Day Lewis for committing 'lamentable ineptitudes while preaching for the cause' (*SLC* 25), while Spender's review of MacNeice's *Poems* implicitly criticizes him for hedging his ideological position: 'he never achieves a crystalline phrase, nor a hard statement'.[30] This underlines the second major difference between the poets in terms of political allegiance. Though all were broadly left wing, MacNeice never became a communist, yet never felt the need to revise his anti-capitalist views.[31] However, there was no simple opposition between the communists on the one side and the non-communists on the other. Spender was among the first to criticize 'Yes, why do we all, seeing a red, feel small?', arguing that it fails precisely 'because a system of thought predominates, and crushes out the spontaneous thought and sympathy of the writer' (*DE* 253). MacNeice could not have stated the poem's problems better.

The poets' self-presentations also offer significant contrasts. Both in *World within World* and his autobiographical poems and fictions, Spender's persona is that of an outsider, misunderstood yet frantic to be accepted. The much anthologized 'My parents kept me from children who were rough' is a case in point. The speaker simultaneously fears the children with 'their muscles like iron/ And their jerking hands and their knees tight on my arms' and longs to join them (*NCP* 8–9). The dynamic of the poem insists both on the children's compelling, violent glamour and his own ineluctable isolation:

> They threw mud
> And I looked another way, pretending to smile.
> I longed to forgive them, yet they never smiled.

The poet-speaker's apartness is absolute. His pretend smile is paired with, but fails to rhyme precisely with, the children's refusal to smile, underlining a conventional separation between the sensitive poetic subject – the locus of sympathy and pathos – and the enigmatic, unyieldingly 'rough' children.

Similarly, Day Lewis, as the most aesthetically conservative of these writers, tends to conventional formulations of the poet's role. 'The Conflict' centres on the question of how the poet should respond to political turmoil. The speaker formerly 'sang as one/ Who on a tilting deck sings/ To keep their courage up'; this develops into a Shelleyan analogy between the poet and a bird: 'As storm-cocks sing,/ Flinging their natural answer in the wind's teeth' (*TD* 11–12).[32] The poem recognizes that such attitudes have become outmoded: though his singing brings him 'peace,/ Above the clouds, outside the ring', the poet lives 'between two massing powers [...]/ Whom neutrality cannot save'. He must fit his singing to revolutionary imperatives, becoming in effect a choirmaster for 'new desires':

> The red advance of life
> Contracts pride, calls out the common blood,
> Beats song into a single blade,
> Makes a depth-charge of grief.

The allegory is clear enough: the traditional poetic role, in which the poet is a self-involved singer, abstracted from 'the common good', must adapt to 'The red advance of life'. The poem shows Day Lewis in the process of convincing himself of his revolutionary obligations, yet its vitality lies precisely in the fact that it fails to resolve the conflict it outlines. Both in its allegory and lush imagery, the poem exhibits the power traditional forms and modes of writing continued to exercise over Day Lewis's imagination. The conventional poetic truism that 'sorrow finds a swift release in song/ And pride its poise' is more convinced, and therefore more convincing, than the rather earnest Stalinism suggested by 'Beats song into a single blade'.

This sense that Spender and Day Lewis are more traditional poets also mirrors the differences between their careers and MacNeice's. Though Day Lewis spent what *The Buried Day* views as eight frustrating years as a prep schoolteacher, by the later 1930s his income from the detective books he wrote under the pseudonym of Nicholas Blake was sufficient to enable him to become a full-time writer.[33] While never rich, Spender had a private income which kept him financially afloat during the 1930s. Afterwards, he worked as the editor of *Horizon* and *Encounter* and, from the 1950s, took up a series of prestigious lectureships in American and British universities. Day Lewis and Spender were largely professional writers. Only for brief periods in their lives were they employees; certainly, there is nothing in their lives to compare with MacNeice's long association with the BBC. Despite the complexity of his relationship with the BBC, in comparison with his peers, it afforded MacNeice a greater level of insight and sympathy with the working lives of ordinary people. Kafka's subject, MacNeice was to write, 'really is Everyman though it is Everyman very much in a twentieth-century context' (*VP* 133). The same is true of MacNeice himself.

2

Modern Hopes:
The Poetry of the 1930s

Few writers have registered the imperative to be (or at least seem) new as intensely as the poets of the 1930s. MacNeice's 'Hidden Ice' begins 'There are few songs for domesticity/ For routine work, money-making or scholarship', then eulogizes those neglected endeavours: 'I would praise our inconceivable stamina/ Who work to the clock and calendar'. Though this praise is modified by 'hidden ice or currents no one noted' which can undermine the most routine lives, this text encapsulates the ambition to expand the subject matter of poetry which was shared by all three writers (CP 89–90). Similar novelty is apparent in Spender's 'The Pylons'.[1] The shock value of this text lies in its lavishing of a traditional style on what was widely perceived as a symbol of the modern brutalization of the English landscape. Spender juxtaposes the aggressive assertiveness of the pylons – 'Bare like nude, giant girls that have no secret' – with the pastoral landscape they have colonized, aligning them with 'the quick perspective of the future' (NCP 21). Whether or not Spender's poem is an unproblematic endorsement of a technological utopia, it implies that modern poetry should address modern subjects. Since poetry is still widely supposed to be a 'green' art form which sides with Nature rather than Technology, 'The Pylons' remains controversial. The next two chapters consider the novelty of the poets of the 1930s. This chapter examines how they responded to and reacted against the prevailing literary culture of their time, and explores the differences of poetic and political outlook in work published between 1933 and 1935.

In surveys of the decade, Samuel Hynes, Bernard Bergonzi and Valentine Cunningham have seen MacNeice as a significant figure, yet one who lacks the centrifugal and period-defining magnetism of Auden. Adrian Caesar's revisionist account sees MacNeice as another Oxbridge bourgeois who contributes to the formulation of an 'Auden myth' which has distracted attention from more politically radical poets like Jack Lindsay and Hugh MacDiarmid.[2] Studies which concentrate on MacNeice have tended, especially in recent years, to emphasize his differences from his English friends and contemporaries. MacNeice's Irishness has become an important issue for the reading of his 1930s poetry. 'Belfast', 'Valediction' and 'Carrickfergus' figure prominently in the work of Terence Brown, Edna Longley and Peter McDonald, who have explored what Brown defines as MacNeice's 'spiritually hyphenated' position between Ireland and England.[3] This work illustrates the problems MacNeice presents to literary history. Should he be seen as a 'professional lacrymose Irishman', as one among many Auden imitators, or as 'a major Anglo-Irish writer rather than as an adjunct to the Auden group'?[4] As I have argued in the previous chapter, the idea of an 'Auden group' is inherently problematic. In the wake of Brown's sense that 'the English MacNeice' has slipped from critical notice, this chapter reconsiders MacNeice's work of the early 1930s alongside that of Spender and Day Lewis, while chapter 3 explores his collaboration with Auden on *Letters from Iceland*.[5] My objective is not to diminish the importance of MacNeice's Irishness – as chapter 4 argues, the tension between 'Irish' and 'British' impulses is crucial to his war poetry. Nevertheless, his relations with his largely English contemporaries were vital to his poetic theory and practice. Though I dissent from the notion that MacNeice was just a cheerleader for Auden, the fact remains that he published in the same periodicals as his English friends, that his criticism continuously engages with their work, and that he co-wrote a book with Auden. Reading MacNeice alongside Spender and Day Lewis enables us to explore the interplay between poetry and period: the ways in which this poetry poeticizes that decade. Moreover, it helps to clarify anew, in the practice of rereading, the relative merits of their work. Edna Longley has fantasized that there will be books with titles like *The MacNeice Generation* and *Thirties*

Poets – The MacNeice Group, noting that 'To turn the tables is not to deny Auden's eminence – only his pre-eminence'.[6] I contribute to this re-evaluation by presenting the decade's poetry with the non-conformist MacNeice at its heart.

The texts discussed in this chapter were selected for complementary reasons. Criticism published between 1934 and 1935 illustrates the often dialogic contrasts between Day Lewis and Spender on the one hand and MacNeice on the other. Poems published during the same time exemplify the intersections between text and period in the ways in which the poets respond to the ambiguities of the historical moment. As Hynes cautions, 'every year of the 'thirties' was 'a year of crises'.[7] I focus on the earlier years of the decade because the three poets published at this time a large amount of poetry and prose – work which established their reputations – and because the threat posed by European dictatorships was becoming clear to left-leaning writers. How should modern poets respond to the times they were living in? In their varied output, all three provide shifting answers to this question.

NEW APPROACHES TO POETRY

Any movement which positions itself as being 'new' presupposes an 'older' tradition against which it reacts. Reaction against the past was an important psychological and rhetorical rite of passage for the poets of the 1930s. For Auden (in journal entries from 1929 which reflect on Freud's death-wish theory), 'The real "life-wish" is the desire for separation, from family, from one's literary predecessors. ... The Tyranny of the Dead. One cannot react against them.'[8] While the Dead cannot be conscious of the reactions of the living, the 'life-wish' pushes Auden to 'separate' from his 'literary predecessors' in the same way as it forces the young adult to separate from his or her family. Similarly, Day Lewis reviews English literary history through the lens of the parable of the prodigal son. In this more comforting model of intergenerational conflict, reaction against tradition is an integral part of the creation of new work:

> In English poetry there have been several occasions on which the younger son, fretting against parental authority, weary of routine

35

work on the home farm [...] has packed his bag and set out for a far country. Rumours of his doings come to our ears: [...] He is flirting with foreign whores [...] he has wasted his fortune: he has forgotten how to speak English: he has shamed his father [...] Only his father smiles indulgently, feeling a secret pride, assured of the vigour of his seed. Then the younger son returns, not a broken prodigal, but healthy, wealthy and wise [...] he has money in the bank, strange tales to tell us, and some fine children already. (*HP* 1)

Where Auden focuses on 'the desire for separation' from the literary and familial past, Day Lewis implies that the history of English poetry is a sequence of fractured yet constitutive father–son relationships in which apparent rebellion ultimately confirms the 'vigour' of the paternal 'seed'. For Day Lewis, poetic 'ancestor-worship' becomes 'the only possible patriotism, the one necessary link with the past, and the meaning of tradition' (*HP* 3).

Auden's journal and *A Hope for Poetry* suggest that much was at stake in the way the poets of the 1930s reacted to their literary forebears. These reactions were more than just matters of literary taste: they are points of cultural and political self-definition. Day Lewis, himself a young father who had lyrically celebrated the birth of his first son in *From Feathers to Iron*, conceives of literary tradition in paternalistic terms. The veneration of English tradition inherent in the parable anticipates the increasing traditionality of Day Lewis's work, which culminated with his appointment as poet laureate in 1968. Conversely, the homosexual Auden notes the tensions between the individual and his predecessors. Though Auden himself would adopt more a conventional political and aesthetic outlook, he never lost the sense that literary and sexual identity is produced through a struggle with the past.[9] Though MacNeice, Spender and Day Lewis had subtly different theories of poetry, the sense of conflict between past and present was common to all three. What then was the poetic culture against which these writers defined themselves, and in what ways did they find it wanting?

The writers' critical works are valuable guides to their responses to recent poetry. Yet the poetic scene which emerges from contemporaneous texts like *A Hope for Poetry*, 'Poetry To-day', and *The Destructive Element* is, to say the least, variegated.[10] As MacNeice observed, 'unlike our more parochial predecessors, we have so many Pasts and Presents to choose from' (*SLC* 14). Even within this socially and educationally homogenous generation of writers, there is no single tradition, nor an agreed reading of the present. Nevertheless, reaction to T. S. Eliot is central to all three. Spender's critique of Eliot's essay 'Tradition and the Individual Talent' (which insists on the necessity of a sense of tradition for the production of any new poetry) articulates the difficulties inherent in the idea of tradition. Eliot ignores 'a sense of tradition [...] derived from the conditions of life round the poet', hence his insensitivity to nature poetry (*DE* 161). In his insistence on the importance of orthodoxy of belief, Eliot's ideas become dangerously congruent with the authoritarianism of Mussolini and Hitler (*DE* 167). Indeed, tradition is never a neutral concept. Day Lewis's 'ancestor-worship' might shade into a submissive veneration of great men; his 'Letter to a Young Revolutionary' (from *New Country*) concludes by approvingly quoting from Lawrence's authoritarian novel *Aaron's Rod*, urging the young man to submit himself to revolutionary discipline. '[T]he submission of a man to his natural leader' was potentially a virtue for left and right alike.[11] Beyond Eliot, *The Destructive Element* focuses on Henry James and his influence on Modernism, arguing that the literature of the twentieth century shows the growing importance of 'a political subject' (*DE* 187). The poetry of Day Lewis and Auden shows the way towards 'a possible Communist literature' (*DE* 251). Spender places his contemporaries alongside James, Yeats, Eliot and Lawrence to suggest that their work is a product of the first wave of Modernism. As a critical study rather than a manifesto, *The Destructive Element* does not describe contemporary poetic fashions in any detail.

Throughout *A Hope for Poetry*, Day Lewis uses the parable of the prodigal son as a means of condensing literary history. Hopkins, Owen and Eliot are singled out as 'our immediate ancestors', as 'younger sons who could not stay at home' (*HP* 3, 6). While conceding that they 'have little else apparently in common', Day Lewis suggests that each poet was technically original and that each was at variance with the culture in which he grew up (*HP* 6). This approach is congruent with Spender's: the three poets become talismanic figures who anticipate the poetry of the 1930s. Yet Day Lewis's response to Eliot has a different emphasis from Spender's. Where Spender saw *The*

Waste Land as an archetypal modern poem whose form mirrors the 'fragmentary world' (*DE* 143), Day Lewis attacked its collage technique on the grounds that it confirmed reactionary expectations of modern poetry (*HP* 22–3). Such scepticism is indicative of a stylistic conservatism which underpins both *A Hope for Poetry* and his own work. Day Lewis's hope for poetry was that modern subject matter, embracing a progressive political outlook, could be combined with the revitalizing of traditional poetic technique.

Other than this literary-historical myth, Day Lewis provides little detail about contemporary poetry. He sidesteps Yeats (a significant presence for both Spender and MacNeice); in a different vein, he is airily dismissive of the Georgian poets:

> a sadly pedestrian rabble, flocked along the roads their fathers had built, pointing out to each other the beauty spots and ostentatiously drinking small-beer in a desperate effort to prove their virility. The winds blew, the floods came: [...] they were rolled under and nothing marks their graves. (*HP* 2)

The Georgians were convenient fall guys: though a poet as radical as Lawrence had been published in the *Georgian Poetry* anthologies which appeared between 1912 and 1922, Georgianism was a conservative movement which fostered pastoral poems, often in praise of the English countryside, in a readily comprehensible poetic idiom.[12] Day Lewis is aggressive partly because of his own insecurity: the accusation that he was a closet Georgian dogged him throughout the decade. Though Georgian-bashing became something of a communal sport during the 1930s (when having a good word for Rupert Brooke was intellectual heresy), MacNeice's essay offers an instructive contrast. Where Day Lewis uses the language of parable to condemn the Georgians without explaining why their work was feeble, MacNeice reads them in the context of nineteenth-century literature:

> A suburban individualism prevailed, the penalty for the bumptious anarchism of the Romantic Revival. The poets of the 'nineties and the Georgians who succeeded them were crippled by a reaction from the prophets; they did not dare to be moral, didactic, propagandist or even intellectual (*SLC* 14–15)

While both writers are anxious to prove their cosmopolitan credentials – the reader could reasonably conclude from these extracts that the modern poet should never walk in the country nor come from the suburbs – MacNeice presents Georgian shortcomings historically. Like the aesthetes of the 1890s, the Georgians were 'crippled' by their reaction against the anarchism of the Romantics, leading to a timorous poetry, self-consciously withdrawn from any substantive contact with the dangerous material of real life. By implication, contemporary poets must dare to take moral and political stances.

Like Day Lewis, MacNeice was sceptical about some of the technical innovations of the Modernists. Though it is an essay rather than a book, 'Poetry To-day' offers a more comprehensive sense of poetic zeitgeist than either *A Hope for Poetry* or *The Destructive Element*. His account of Modernism goes beyond Eliot and Yeats, taking in American poetry and showing some familiarity with French writing. He discusses the Sitwells, Graves and Riding, mentioning works as diverse as Wyndham Lewis's *One-Way Song* and Hugh MacDiarmid's *A Drunk Man Looks at the Thistle*. From this perspective, MacNeice offers another perspective on Eliot:

> All these poets, Pound, Graves, Riding, Cummings, and the Sitwells, have been admirably adventurous and ingenious, but, as far as living tradition is concerned, they are so many blind alleys. [...] To find a bridge between the dominant poetry of the early nineteen-twenties and the dominant poetry of the early nineteen-thirties we have to look back again to T. S. Eliot. [...] For this general movement towards clarity and rigour Mr Eliot is largely responsible (*SLC* 21–2)

Though the essay later warns that *The Waste Land* 'cannot become a practical classic, i.e. a classic which the next poets shall use as a model', Eliot remains central to MacNeice's sense of how English poetry has developed: 'For me the history of post-War poetry in England is the history of Eliot and the reaction from Eliot' (*SLC* 40, 39). In contrast to Day Lewis, who saw Eliot as a reactionary father figure who ought to set his sons a better example (*HP* 23–5), MacNeice's Eliot is a genuinely innovative poet who managed to turn the experimentalism of the first generation of Modernists into an idiosyncratic yet influential poetry and who – paradoxically in the light of Eliot's own theories – contributed to a movement in the 1930s 'towards clarity and rigour'.[13]

Collectively, these texts point to the dividing line between traditional styles rooted in the poetry of the nineteenth century and avant-garde writing which appeared more in tune with the realities of post-war experience. For all three, *The Waste Land* is a watershed between the past and the present. All in their different ways side with Eliot's poem against the forces of aesthetic reaction. Yet as MacNeice quipped in 1961 about his tastes as a young man, there was a sense in which the admiration of Eliot was mandatory for any upwardly mobile young poet: 'While one *had* to admire *The Waste Land*, one *could* not have been seen reading Galsworthy' (*Prose*, 232). To the poets of the 1930s, the Georgians embodied the unthinkable Galsworthy. Yet despite the fact that 'one' had to dismiss the Georgians, both 'Poetry To-day' and *A Hope for Poetry* exhibit residual admiration for traditional techniques alongside scepticism about the method of *The Waste Land*.

Moreover, the conflict between modernity and tradition was not a simple choice in which the aesthetic mirrored the political. As Spender's analysis of Eliot's cult of tradition indicates, the Modernists tended to be politically conservative if not actually sympathetic towards fascism. MacDiarmid was the only significant writer of the previous generation to espouse communism, and as Day Lewis pointed out, 'Most of his poetry is written in the Scots vernacular, which may account for [its] neglect in England' (*HP* 50–1). This is a useful reminder of the parochialism both of the writers themselves and their broader literary culture. These accounts of twentieth-century poetry are all tendentious in that they are concerned to open up a space where the poets' own work and the work of their colleagues seem like an inevitable advance on the poetry of the preceding generation. In resisting the tyranny of the dead and middle-aged, they construct a self-constituting oligarchy, which effaces the differences between individual writers and which attempts to position them as the legitimate yet rebellious offspring of Eliot.

Yet, as chapter 1 argued, there was little political consensus between Day Lewis, Spender and MacNeice. Their poetics are aligned in the broad sense that poetry should be concerned with contemporary politics, and in the recognition of Auden as a new voice whose work embodied this movement towards 'a political subject'. Though Day Lewis and Spender were prepared to adapt their poetry to their politics, there were significant disjunctions in their thinking. Spender's 'Poetry and Revolution' (from *New Country*) begins with the admission that writing poetry is 'one of the least revolutionary' activities, insisting that 'The artist cannot renounce the bourgeois tradition because the proletariat has no alternative tradition which he could adopt'. The essay articulates the very real difficulties Spender felt in 'adopting' a Communist perspective. Anticipating the tentative optimism of Auden's *Oxford Book of Light Verse*, Spender concludes that 'by making clear the causes of our present frustration [individualist writers] may prepare the way for a new kind of society'.[14] The tension remains: as an upper-middle-class poet, Spender drew imaginative sustenance from the 'bourgeois tradition'. While Day Lewis acknowledged these difficulties, in an essay published in the Communist journal *Left Review* in 1935, the recognition that the 'tradition of poetry' has been 'developed by a dominating class' is guided by the injunction that the poet should 'not think of poetry as a mystery whose secret is only held by the educated bourgeois' but should compel 'an alien tradition into his own service, just as the U.S.S.R. pressed the industrial technique of capitalist Europe into the service of Socialism'.[15] The essay shows Day Lewis in the act of proving his political orthodoxy: in this analogy, poetry is 'pressed' into industrial service as it submits to revolutionary discipline. 'Poetry To-day' casts a withering eye over such attitudes:

> I have no patience with those who think poetry [...] will be merely a handmaid of communism. Christianity, in the time of the Fathers, made the same threats; all poetry but hymns was bogus, no one was to write anything but hymns. (*SLC* 25)

The passage continues with the caveat that 'intoxication with a creed is [...] a good antidote to defeatist individualism'. MacNeice was hostile to naïve progressive idealism and to the suggestion manifest in Day Lewis's essay that the autonomy of the poet should be harnessed to the demands of the cause. But he shared his colleagues' sense that poetry should be more politically engaged than it had been.

In comparing these texts, it becomes apparent that the major distinction between MacNeice and the others is in their attitudes to the function of poetry. Though neither Spender nor Day

Lewis advocated a completely propagandist theory of literature, their critical writings of the mid-1930s mark the moment at which left-leaning intellectuals tried to adapt their bourgeois education to revolutionary idealism. The titles of the essays are revealing: 'Poetry and Revolution', 'Revolutionaries and Poetry' as against 'Poetry To-day'. Spender and Day Lewis were as much concerned with articulating their position in relation to revolutionary politics as they were in expounding their poetics. In contrast, MacNeice's central interest was with poetry itself: he never puts politics on an equal footing with poetry, nor does he try to adapt his faith in poetry to the exigencies of any competing ideology. The contrast between the aspirant radicalism of Spender and Day Lewis and the sceptical yet politically alert position of MacNeice underpins the poetry the three produced during the 1930s.

'TO WILL THIS TIME'S CHANGE'

Day Lewis

As these poets were preoccupied with the need to appear modern, so their poetry circulated around the problem of how to interpret the times in which they were living. Though Day Lewis and Spender later repudiated communism, the early 1930s were a period of political polarization and economic catastrophe throughout Europe. Recession in Britain made at least two and a half million men unemployed by the end of 1931. The collapse of the first Labour government in the same year, and the subsequent election of a conservative 'national' government fronted by former Labour prime minister Ramsay MacDonald, seemed to signal the death of constitutional socialism. Nearly ten years later MacNeice lambasted 'the deplorable trinity of MacDonald, Jimmy Thomas and Snowden' (who left Labour to form the 'national' government) with a disdain which communicates the depth of the betrayal felt by the left: these men had 'sold their birthright' (*SF* 135). In such circumstances, communism offered a plausible alternative. Day Lewis's 'Learning to Talk', the first poem in *A Time to Dance* (1935), initially seems remote from such events. It contrasts a small child's understanding of time with that of the speaker:

[...] He can't contain
The exquisite moment overflowing.
Limbs leaping, woodpecker flying
Are for him and not hereafter.

Tongue trips, recovers, triumphs,
Turning all ways to express
What the forward eye can guess –
That time is his and earth young.

We are growing too like trees
To give the rising wind a voice:
Eagles shall build upon our verse,
Our winged seeds are to-morrow's sowing.

Yes, we learn to speak for all
Whose hearts here are not at home,
All who march to a better time
And breed the world for which they burn.

(TD 7)

'Learning to Talk' illustrates Day Lewis's compromise between poetic ambition, his enthusiasm for communism and the desire to appear modern. Auden's influence is visible in the use of asyndeton, elisions ('Limbs leaping, woodpecker flying' and 'Tongue trips', where the suppression of definite articles and pronouns accelerates the rhythm and conveys a conversational aura) and half rhymes. MacNeice worried that his colleagues used the latter 'indiscriminately and therefore viciously', yet here technique meshes with content (*SLC* 33). As the poem describes the child's hesitant attempts to speak, so the rhymes mimic the iterative processes of language acquisition, in which at one moment 'Tongue trips' and at the next it 'triumphs', when child and reader are rewarded with the only full rhyme in this passage, 'express' and 'guess'. The rhyme implies that learning the structures of human expression is a form of inspired guesswork.

Alongside such modish touches, the poem betrays Day Lewis's adherence to older strategies. At the moment when the poet-speaker generalizes from the description of the child, Day Lewis adopts an inflated and abstract poetic idiom as he seeks to draw a moral from the child's behaviour. For all its technical precision,[16] the poem's analogy between 'learning to talk' and the poet's revolutionary utterance slides into the idiom waspishly mocked by Orwell: 'It is pure scoutmaster, the exact note of the ten-minutes' straight talk on the dangers of self-abuse'.[17] The conflation of abstract imagery with an earnest, moralizing tone makes the revolution seem a rather joylessly worthy prospect, the desirability of which the speaker needs to keep reminding himself: '*We* are growing too like trees [...] *Yes*, we learn to speak'.[18]

'Learning to Talk' is congruent with the attitudes expressed in Day Lewis's prose. As a poem of revolutionary optimism, it insists that there will be 'a better time' in the future. It almost too neatly embodies the advice of 'Revolutionaries and Poetry' in its attempt to force traditional lyricism to the service of the new political message. Yet the poem's sense of the present is dominated by the lyrical description of the child immersed in 'The exquisite moment': the shortcomings of the contemporary world emerge only through the speaker's scoutmasterly reminders of 'all/ Whose hearts here are not at home'. The shortfall between the poet's bourgeois milieu and the external world he wants to remind himself of is palpable; it's hardly surprising that the poem is most imaginatively engaged in describing the child.

Spender

If 'Learning to Talk' articulates a lyrical version of Marxist historiography – in which revolution is an inevitable though not precisely timetabled outcome of the injustices of capitalism – Spender's 'In railway halls' lyrically turns against the procedures of poetry as it seeks to condemn injustice:

> In railway halls, on pavements near the traffic,
> They beg, their eyes made big by empty staring
> And only measuring Time, like the blank clock.
>
> No, I shall weave no tracery of pen-ornament
> To make them birds upon my singing-tree:
> Time merely drives these lives which do not live
> As tides push rotten stuff along the shore.
>
> – There is no consolation, no, none
> In the curving beauty of that line
> Traced on our graphs through history, where the oppressor
> Starves and deprives the poor.

> (*NCP* 22–3)

Spender's poet-speaker also obtrudes his own concerns into the poem. 'No, I shall weave *no* tracery of pen-ornament'; 'There is *no* consolation, *no, none*': the accumulating negatives are as rhetorically impressive as Day Lewis's affirmation is feeble.[19] Spender's interjections convey the intensity of the moral revulsion of the artist against art. This revulsion is visible in the physical shape of the poem: the first three lines form a single, descriptive triplet written in roughly regular iambic pentameter. After the speaker's interjection in the fourth line, rhythm and line length become less predictable. Though it settles into edgy, unrhyming quatrains, the poem depends on the reader's recognition that its last twelve lines react against the form and content of its first three. Spender meditates on the ethics of lyric poetry, reflecting on the tension between the practice of poetry and the realities of poverty. As he refuses to make his subjects 'birds upon my singing-tree', so he constructs an attack on 'the oppressor' which is convincing because poetry itself is held in contempt as a form of 'consolation' and for its attempt to exploit the unemployed for aesthetic purposes. This is particularly evident in the third stanza, where the placement of line breaks cajoles the reader into initially thinking that 'the curving beauty of that line' applies to the poem itself. As we read on it becomes clear that this startling phrase applies to the oppressor's demographic statistics; nevertheless the suggestion of an uncomfortable rapprochement between 'our graphs through history' and the 'pen-ornament' of poetry persists.

Like 'Learning to Talk', 'In railway halls' is preoccupied with time, but not as a purposive or progressive force. Initially, it measures the lives of the unemployed 'like the blank clock', then becomes a tidal force which 'merely drives these lives which do not live'. Finally, the inadequacies of 'This Time' are conflated with those of poetry:

> Paint here no draped despairs, no saddening clouds
> Where the soul rests, proclaims eternity.
> But let the wrong cry out as raw as wounds
> This Time forgets and never heals, far less transcends.

As Michael O'Neill and Gareth Reeves suggest, 'The poem comes face to face with "This Time" – or with the problems of writing about it appropriately'.[20] 'In railway halls' addresses the tension between a sense of the injustices of 'This Time' and the failure of poetry to make anything more than 'draped despairs' from its political subject. While recognizing that poetry cannot ameliorate, the speaker pleads that 'the wrong' itself should 'cry out as raw as wounds'. Paradoxically, although 'This Time' is unable to heal to transcend injustice, the plea imagines the force of the articulate wrong transcending both time and the short-comings of poetry. It is a rhetorical and self-conscious gesture wholly in keeping with the febrile, excitable character of the rest of the poem.

In its avoidance of the determinism of 'Learning to Talk', 'In railway halls' is both a less ideologically orthodox poem and a more successful attempt at rendering contemporary political issues into a distinctively modern poetry. Like many of the best texts in Spender's *Poems*, it manages to be both an almost sociological rendering of the economic slump of the early 1930s and a lyrical encapsulation of a particular habit of mind. Spender's attitude to the present moment in the rest of *Poems* is closer to Day Lewis's than this poem suggests. Poems like 'oh young men oh young comrades', 'The Funeral', 'The Express' (all previewed in *New Signatures*), 'Not palaces' and 'After they have tired of the brilliance of cities' provide rhapsodic vistas on a brighter future:

> Oh comrades, step beautifully from the solid wall
> advance to rebuild and sleep with friend on hill
> advance to rebel and remember what you have
> no ghost ever had, immured in his hall.

> (*NCP* 16)

If Day Lewis sounds like a scoutmaster, Spender's more heterogeneous poetic idiom – mixing verse forms borrowed from Eliot and Lawrence, Shelleyan diction, with soft-core Marxism – sweetens the challenge of rebellion with an orgiastic anticipation of a better, even sexier, world. In contrast with Day Lewis's moral earnestness, this poem insinuates that the 'comrades' will be more sexually successful once they 'advance to rebel'. 'After they have tired of the brilliance of cities' coyly shifts from its assertion of 'The palpable and obvious love of man for men' to the suggestion that the revolutionaries' children will be born through a sort of parthenogenesis as

'The beautiful generation that shall spring from our sides' (*NCP* 18). At one level, such poems could be seen as 'Rupert Brookeian gush'.[21] Yet Spender's conflation of a surreptitious, barely acknowledged homoeroticism with revolutionary rhetoric does at the very least respond to the imperative to innovate.

The form of Spender's verse differs from the more traditional forms favoured by Day Lewis. O'Neill and Reeves have characterized the stanzaic structures of Spender's work as being 'held open to the often ragged mass of feeling; tentative and exploratory, they are concerned to mirror the emergence into words of consciousness'.[22] While this is a useful evocation of the impact of poems like 'In railway halls', where stanzaic shape and line length fluctuate to reflect the speaker's quicksilver emotions, Spender's free verse conveys the excitement of revolutionary fervour more intensely than the work of any of his contemporaries. The final text in *Poems*, 'Not palaces', rejects the aristocratic past in favour of an egalitarian future:

> Not palaces, an era's crown
> Where the mind dwells, intrigues, rests;
> The architectural gold-leaved flower
> From people ordered like a single mind,
> I build. This only what I tell:
> It is too late for rare accumulation,
> For family pride, for beauty's filtered dusts;
> I say, stamping the words with emphasis,
> Drink from here energy and only energy,
> As from the electric charge of a battery,
> To will this Time's change.

> > (*NCP* 25)

Stressing the outmodedness of the past in a language which acknowledges its seductiveness, Spender insists on 'the electric charge' of the present and the new political order which new technologies prefigure. Repeatedly modulating rhythm and line length, Spender's poem has the vertiginous effect of conveying a brutally simple message in a complex poetic language. Note the syntax and lineation of the first sentence, where the active verb is delayed until the end of the period. This has the effect of juxtaposing the passive verbs of the past, 'Where the mind dwells, intrigues, rests', with the vibrant assertion of the present: 'I build'. Spender's commitment to a better future is visible in his syntax: 'I build', indeed, conflates the construction of such a future with the writing of the poem. Spender's revolution remains rooted in the Romantic ideal of the poet as a social prophet. Though 'Not palaces' strikes revolutionary poses, it conveys little practical sense of the revolutionary work Auden would infamously characterize as 'the expending of powers/ On the flat ephemeral pamphlet and the boring meeting'.[23] Nevertheless, the poem's blend of revolutionary forecast and denunciation with syntactic and rhythmic innovation help to explain the critical success of the volume.[24] As Spender 'will[s] this Time's change', the poem emphatically endorses the poet's self-assertion, 'stamping the words with emphasis' in such a way that for the space that we read the poem, its optimism seems not only tangible but reasonable.

Two months after the second expanded edition of *Poems* appeared in September 1934, Spender published a long poem which was not to be reprinted until seventy years later. *Vienna* was almost universally attacked by reviewers, and seems even to have been regarded as something of an embarrassment by Eliot and Faber, because of both its militant politics and its sexualized language.[25] On the first page, a character is described as 'Our wet dream dictator'; later Spender empathetically describes 'Those who hang about/ At jaws of lavatories, advertising their want of love' (*NCP* 49, 67). Yet, as John Sutherland suggests, the poem anticipates the growing intersection between literature and politics: 'Like Madrid two years later, Vienna was, in summer 1934, where European history was being made'.[26] Spender's poem evokes the events of 1934, when the right-wing dictatorship of the Heimwehr party (led by Dollfüss, Stahremberg and Fey) brutally suppressed a socialist rebellion, leading to the deaths of around 2,000 people. The third section 'The Death of Heroes' is a roll-call for those victims. The execution of Wallisch is vividly reported through the voice of his fellow prisoners:

> [...] 56 soldiers
> Armed to the teeth looked rather ridiculous
> To guard 1 man. But we were watching
> From all our cells, prison cells, cells of labour,
> Our leader. They brought him out in a hurry
> For Dollfuss had phoned through to complain of the delay;
> Dollfuss, Dollfuss said 'Hang him low'.

Wallisch stood on the platform and before he died
'Live Socialism', and 'Hail Freedom', he said.
The word 'Freedom' was choked by the rope.

(NCP 62)

This section embodies the poetry theorized by Day Lewis as Spender ventriloquizes the language of class solidarity. Though the texture of the verse lacks the syntactic buoyancy and excitement of poems like 'Not palaces', the seriousness of the events described and the implicit claim they make on the consciousness of the reader is manifest. Wallisch's heroic dignity as a single man guarded by '56 soldiers/ Armed to the teeth' underlines the contrast between socialist martyrs and their oppressors. If Isherwood's autobiographical novel *Mr Norris Changes Trains* (1935) uses the Nazis' rise to power in Berlin as an unsettling backdrop to its otherwise comic tale of the scams and sexual misadventures of Arthur Norris, Spender foregrounds Austrian politics as a matter of urgent relevance to his British readers.

Yet as Spender's later comments reveal, *Vienna* is complicated by being more than a report from the European frontline. He notes that he 'tried to relate the public passion' of his opposition to fascism to his 'private life':

> In part [*Vienna*] expressed my indignation at the suppression of the Viennese Socialists [...] but in part also it was concerned with a love relationship. I meant to show that the two experiences were different, yet related [...] The poem fails because it does not fuse the two halves of a split situation, and attain a unity where the inner passion becomes inseparable from the outer one. (*WW* 191–2)

Spender might have gone further. His affair with Muriel Gardiner, the poem's dedicatee and a committed supporter of Austrian socialism, competed with his on/ off relationship with his secretary and working-class protégé, Tony Hyndman. As Hynes notes, Spender was 'a young man living a troubled and emotional private life, and elements of that life are also part of [*Vienna*]'.[27] The overlap between the private and the political, the uneasy combination of guilt, sex and outrage, underpin the poem. Though Auden had suggested in dedicating *The Orators* to Spender that 'Private faces in public places/ Are wiser and nicer/ Than public faces in private places',[28] the convolutions of

49

Vienna suggest that, however wise and nice as an individual, as a poet, Spender could not reconcile the private with the public:

> We breathe the bandaged air and watch through windows
> Metal limbs, glass eyes, ourselves frozen on fires.
>
> Unless indeed we stand upon a word,
> Forgiveness, the brink of a renewing river...
>
> A word, a brink, like the first uttered love.
> Upon the pulsing throat springs the hot tiger.
> Instantly released, in joy and sorrow they fall,
> Escaping the whole world, two separate worlds of one,
> Writing a new world with their figure 2.
> Accepting the dreaded, the whispered happy postures
> They dive into their dream with dreamed of gestures.
>
> (*NCP* 51)

The difficulty of the writing is symptomatic of Spender's debt to Eliot and Auden as well as the lack of clarity in the poem's design. In this extract, shifts of scene and mood are virtually unsignalled, except through the ellipsis which partially prepares the reader to switch from one 'brink' to another. The first paragraph aptly conveys the atmosphere of a divided city, but by the third paragraph, the focus has shifted to the elliptical description of the start of an affair. Poetically, not to say ideologically, the result is as confusing as it is enlightening. Though the evocation of the lovers 'Escaping the whole world' through 'whispered happy postures' is poetically rich, the text gives no sense of how this erotic idyll might square with events on the streets of Vienna. Should the reader endorse, decry or simply relish this apparent denial of external reality? This passage is symptomatic of *Vienna*'s stylistic ambition and political confusion; the reader must negotiate two sections of such writing before getting to the relative clarity of 'The Death of Heroes'.

In his generous reading of the poem, Hynes maintains that 'The problems of writing *personally* about political events in which one has played no part are very considerable'.[29] For Hynes, as for Spender himself, *Vienna* fails because of the incompatibility between Spender's love life and the Viennese uprising. In this view, Spender could not make either topic significant enough to write a Modernist poem in the tradition of *The Orators* or *The Waste Land*, both of which it resembles, or clear enough to work as effective propaganda. This suggests that *Vienna* was a dead end; yet MacNeice's comments in 'Poetry Today' highlight the poem's experimental value:

> [*Vienna* is] Unsuccessful, I think (still too *voulu*) but the right kind of experiment. I expect poets in the near future to write longer works (epics, epyllia, verse, essays and autobiographies) which will, for the intelligent reader, supersede the stale and plethoric novel. (*SLC* 42)

Though MacNeice's anti-novelistic fighting talk now seems rather dated, his sympathetic response to *Vienna* foreshadows the writing of *Autumn Journal*. He suggests that the problem with Spender's poem is not so much its design – it is 'the right kind of experiment' – but the fact that it is too '*voulu*', a term which conveys the strain of the writing and the earnest deliberation of its political message. MacNeice's diagnosis gives no sense that the personal and the political should not mix. As we shall see, his own longer poems make similar connections between these realms. But MacNeice's personal concerns were expressed more directly than Spender's had been: his experience manages to overlap with both public events and the concerns of his readers.

IN AN EVIL TIME: ESCAPISM AND PLURALITY IN MacNEICE'S *POEMS*

Early readers of MacNeice's *Poems* would have been unlikely to have accused its author of revolutionary zeal. The first lines of its opening poem, 'An Eclogue for Christmas' (*CP* 3–7), are strikingly pessimistic:

> A. I meet you in an evil time.
> B.   The evil bells
> Put out of our heads, I think, the thought of everything else.
> A. The jaded calendar revolves,
> Its nuts need oil, carbon chokes the valves,
> The excess sugar of a diabetic culture
> Rotting the nerve of life and literature;
> Therefore when we bring out the old tinsel and frills
> To announce that Christ is born among the barbarous hills
> I turn to you whom a morose routine
> Saves from the mad vertigo of being what has been.

Though I have already queried Day Lewis's suggestion that *Poems* embodies 'a return to the ideals of poetic integrity and artistic individualism', it is easy to see why he read poems like 'An Eclogue' in this way (*HP* 80). The city dwelling speaker (A) and the countryman (B) present a bleak assessment of the future unleavened by revolutionary optimism: 'the whore and the buffoon/ Will come off best; no dreamers, they cannot lose their dream/ And are at least likely to be reinstated in the new régime'. In this context, Spender's aspiration 'To will this Time's change' seems merely wilful: 'dreamers' of his kind ignore the *realpolitik* in which the 'new régime' re-employs the same flunkeys as the old. In the opening exchange, the speakers diagnose the ailments 'of a diabetic culture', in which the prospect of Christmas is another 'morose routine' of 'old tinsel and frills'. It is difficult to see MacNeice as 'returning' to anything. The consummate technical skill of the opening lies in the way it evokes but subverts the traditional forms of pastoral eclogue and heroic rhyming couplet. MacNeice's consciously slovenly, consciously 'jazzy' couplets, with their 'jaded' half rhymes ('revolves'/ 'valves') and their uncertain line length (the second line stretches to a lazy fourteen syllables followed by a weary hemistich of eight) give the text the illusion of a traditional structure. But as the celebration of Christmas is a traditional reflex no longer ballasted by belief, so the mutable form of the couplet illustrates the 'Rotting [...] nerve of life and literature'. Traditional forms are still available, but they carry no conviction or authority.

The poem's handling of modern cultural forms is equally underwhelmed. Jazz insistently underscores A's alienation: his generation is 'Jazz-weary of years of drums and Hawaiian guitar' and 'planked and panelled with jazz'. It is a 'jaded music' which forms a soundtrack by which 'To forswear thought and become an automaton'. Neither tradition nor innovation provide any convincing cultural vocabulary which might stabilize the speakers' drifting identities. The speakers give the impression of masquerading as the Arcadian shepherds of classical pastoral; their sense of their own identity has virtually disintegrated. A sees himself 'sifted and splintered in broken facets' in the increased fracturing of the human subject in modern art; B elegizes the decay of rural England:

In the country they are still hunting, in the heavy shires
Greyness is on the fields and sunset like a line of pyres
Of barbarous heroes smoulders through the ancient air
Hazed with factory dust and, orange opposite, the moon's glare,
Goggling yokel-stubborn through the iron trees,
Jeers at the end of us, our bland ancestral ease;
We shall go down like palaeolithic man
Before some new Ice Age or Genghiz Khan.

In contrast to Spender's technological optimism, B sees the growth of 'the iron trees' of modern factories as anticipating the end of traditional lifestyles 'in the heavy shires'. That 'they are still hunting' underlines the obsolescence of this 'bland' aristocracy, comfortable with its 'ancestral ease' but impervious to the realities of social and economic change, or to the political threat of a 'new [...] Genghiz Khan'. The poem is fundamentally concerned with the way in which traditions, whether of hunting or of writing poetry, can disguise the true dimensions of this 'evil time'. As B observes, 'everywhere the pretence of individuality recurs': 'The excess sugar of a diabetic culture' is revealed in the failure to recognize the hollowness of traditions and the sickly-sweet corruption of the present moment. This is why the speakers are given those cryptic, anonymizing tags: they are not individuals, they are figures that represent the erosion of individuality, who namelessly voice the divided plight of the modern everyman.

The literary politics of *Poems* are complicated: while 'An Eclogue for Christmas' resists progressive optimism, the same poem sees little hope in individualism either. Such tensions are evident in two texts which, in *Poems*, are printed on adjacent pages, 'Turf-stacks' and 'The Individualist Speaks'. These poems are usually seen as embodiments of MacNeice's suspicion of communism.[30] According to such views, 'Turf-stacks' (*CP* 15–16) juxtaposes a positive pastoral landscape with a negative image of an industrial city. Yet the detail of the poem, as well as its original coupling with 'The Individualist Speaks', suggests that other perspectives are in the play:

Among these turf-stacks graze no iron horses
Such as stalk, such as champ in towns and the soul of crowds,
Here is no mass-production of neat thoughts
No canvas shrouds for the mind nor any black hearses:

> The peasant shambles on his boots like hooves
> Without thinking at all or wanting to run in grooves.

While the pastoral landscape is preferred to the 'iron' city, the peasant is reduced in the couplet to a human horse who 'shambles [...]/ Without thinking at all'. The second stanza presents what is usually seen as MacNeice's attack on communist intellectuals: 'those who lack the peasant's conspirators [...]/ Will feel the need of a fortress against ideas and against the/ Shuddering insidious shock of the theory-vendors'. Though these lines are congruent with the attack in 'Poetry To-day' on the view that poetry 'will become the handmaid of communism', the speaker of 'Turf-stacks' is indiscriminately hostile to 'theory' and 'ideas' alike:

> For we are obsolete who like the lesser things
> Who play in corners with looking-glasses and beads;
> It is better we should go quickly; go into Asia
> Or any other tunnel where the world recedes,
> Or turn blind wantons like the gulls who scream
> And rip the edge off any ideal or dream.

The speaker's escapism is explicit. He concedes the obsolescence of his class, languidly imagines a retreat into Asia, and a final transformation of such aesthetes into 'blind wantons' who 'rip the edge off any ideal or dream'. 'Turf-stacks' envisages the speaker's detachment resolving into the screaming, destructive cynicism of 'the gulls'. MacNeice's suspicion of anti-intellectualism suggests that the speaker is a Bloomsbury-ite aesthete, resistant to the notion that poetry should have intellectual content.[31] Quoting the final stanza, Day Lewis suggested 'His attitude to life is one of humorous but armed neutrality' (*HP* 82). This paradox provides a helpful way of understanding the poem: while it seems 'armed' against 'the theory-vendors', it is lethargically 'neutral' towards escapism. This is MacNeice's point: disengaged escapists are, on their own admission, 'obsolete'.

The subject of 'The Individualist Speaks' is also an escapist, or more precisely an escapee: '– But I will escape, with my dog, on the far side of the Fair' (*CP* 16). This evocative line, exactly pitched between a boast and a threat, is the speaker's response to 'Avenging youth threatening an old war' which will 'scale off masks and smash the purple lights' of the Fair which the

Individualist inhabits. Like 'Turf-stacks', the poem initially seems to endorse its speaker's resistance to social and intellectual upheaval. Yet, as McDonald observes, 'nothing is known about the Individualist's way of escape; he seems to be left deeper in isolation'.[32] The close of the poem is left open as the reader has to make sense of this final gesture. The almost comic detail of the dog may have disposed readers, aware of MacNeice's own predilections (he is one of few modern poets to have shown dogs at Crufts), too hurriedly in the protagonist's favour. In *Autumn Journal*, MacNeice's dog is mocked as 'a symbol of the abandoned order', an 'inept and glamorous' would-be film star with acquisitive appetites: dogs, it seems, are as various as their owners (*CP* 102). The activities associated with the Fair are hedonistic and destructive: 'We [...]/ Are always cowardly and never sober'; 'we/ Knock our brains together extravagantly/ Instead of planting them to make more trees'. This image recalls MacNeice's definition of communism in his review of *The Destructive Element*: 'Communism in the truer sense is an effort to think, and think into action, human society as an organism (*not* a machine, which is too static a metaphor)' (*SLC* 6). The Individualist scorns the sort of 'organic' activity MacNeice advocated. Despite the glamour of his non-conformity, the Individualist is, like the sensibility explored in 'Turf-stacks', opposed to any attempts to 'think into action, human society as an organism'.

Though the text leaves the provenance of the Fair enigmatic, I suggest that it alludes to Vanity Fair, the great market of commercial and moral corruption in *Pilgrim's Progress*. The Individualist and his cronies lack the virtue of sobriety which is ascribed to Christian and Faithful within the Fair: 'the men were quiet, and sober, and intended no body any harm'.[33] Read in this context, the Individualist becomes a dealer in the kind of exploitative market excoriated by Bunyan, a purveyor of 'feathery' commercial fripperies like 'steam-organs, thigh-rub and cream soda'. His recognition that 'A prophet scanning the road on the hither hills/ Might utter the old warning of the old sin' recalls Bunyan's denunciation of Vanity Fair. Though this may suggest too earnest an approach to the poem, my point is not that MacNeice replicates the moralizing strategies of Bunyan, but that he positions the Individualist in such a way

55

as to suggest that his neutrality is not politically innocent. Indeed, it is the Individualist's neutrality, like that of the speaker of 'Turf-stacks', which makes him suspect. The poem's final line simultaneously asserts the Individualist's hardiness and warns that he *will* escape. The reforming project of the 'Avenging youth' will not snare the Individualist, who remains at large 'on the far side of the Fair'.

As these poems demonstrate, MacNeice's approach to the 'political subject' was different from, and often critical of, Day Lewis and Spender's.[34] Yet *Poems* is no more reactive than it is individualistic. Many of the poems exhibit both an interest in ordinary living and a resistance to 'bourgeois' values and routines. 'Ode' (*CP* 37) mocks 'the houses where parents/ Have reared their children to be parents' in the middle-class surroundings of 'Cut box and privet'; 'Sunday Morning' (*CP* 21) begins with a comic vignette of the bourgeoisie at play: 'Man's heart expands to tinker with his car/ For this is Sunday morning, Fate's great bazaar'. Although mockery of middle-class mores is congruent with the attitudes displayed in *The Strings are False*, *Poems* shows the crucial realization that the everyday could become a compelling poetic subject. 'Snow' (*CP* 24) celebrates 'The drunkenness of things being various' through the juxtaposition of 'Spawning snow and pink roses' and the eating of a tangerine in the same moment. Despite its apparent surrealism, as MacNeice explained, the poem 'means exactly what it says [...] in my window was a jar of pink roses and outside the window it had just begun to snow. I suddenly felt how strange – and exciting – it was that all these things should be going on at once'. This 'sudden and intense realisation of the obvious' leads to a series of inlaid aphorisms: 'World is suddener than we fancy it'; 'World is crazier and more of it than we think/ Incorrigibly plural'; 'world/ Is more spiteful and gay than one supposes'.[35] Each intensifier rebukes the speaker's assumptions: that the world is neither sudden, crazy, spiteful nor gay. Through poetic self-correction, MacNeice enriches the perception of ordinary experience.

That the world is 'more spiteful [...] than one supposes' points to the fact that MacNeice's plurality was more than a liberal acknowledgement of diversity. The spite which 'Snow' uncovers gestures towards a broader recognition that 'world' is inherently unpredictable and unstable. 'Nature Morte' (*CP* 23) explores the dimensions of the ordinary through its evocation of middle-class living and its reflections on still lifes, which in turn uncomfortably reflect the forms through which people structure their lives. Like 'Snow', the poem interweaves the familiar with the enigmatic:

> As those who are not athletic at breakfast day by day
> Employ and enjoy the sinews of others vicariously,
> Shielded by the upheld journal from their dream-puncturing wives
> And finding in the printed word a multiplication of their lives,
> So we whose senses give us things misfelt and misheard
> Turn also, for our adjustment, to the pretentious word
> Which stabilises the light on sun-fondled trees
> And, by photographing our ghosts, claims to put us at our ease

MacNeice evokes middle-class men reading the sports pages: the 'journal' shields them from 'their dream-puncturing wives'; reading about 'the sinews of others' distracts them from their sedentary occupations and their role as employers. This momentary escape from reality connects the unathletic men with the 'we' of the fifth line. The simile explains that as the men shield themselves by reading the sports pages, so these speakers try to 'adjust' and 'stabilise' experience through their reliance on 'the pretentious word'. The last four lines juxtapose the speakers' photographic, not to say pedantic, 'reconstructions' of 'our ghosts' with still lifes:

> Yet even so, no matter how solid and staid we contrive
> Our reconstructions, even a still life is alive
> And in your Chardin the appalling unrest of the soul
> Exudes from the dried fish and the brown jug and the bowl.

Since the speakers want to be put at their ease through 'solid and staid' photographs, still lifes would seem to be their ideal formal medium, in which, as in the French title, nature is represented through dead or inorganic objects. But 'your Chardin', despite its ostensibly 'dead' subject matter, relentlessly betrays 'the appalling unrest of the soul'; as the subtitle warns '*Even so it is not so easy to be dead*'. At one level, the poem rehearses attitudes MacNeice had adopted at Marlborough under the tutelage of Anthony Blunt and, indirectly, Roger Fry: 'we had swallowed Significant Form and were strenuously trying to dissociate paintings from their representational content' (*SF* 234). For MacNeice, Significant Form was always a pose in tension with his actual response to 'Chardin's dull brown loaves': 'We may have asked him for an abstract, but by God he gives us bread'.[36] 'Nature Morte' refuses to read Chardin's 'dried fish and the brown jug and the bowl' as formal properties only: the painted forms refer to real objects. Yet the poem is more than a satiric gloss on art historical theory. Through its evocation of bourgeois routines and its responsiveness to 'the appalling unrest of the soul' in the representation of domestic interiors, 'Nature Morte' displays MacNeice's quickening sense of his own subject matter. The 'still life' is paradoxically 'alive'; it is neither static nor stable.

As 'Snow' re-evaluates static preconceptions, so this poem critically explores attempts to stabilize and reconstruct experience. While both bear witness to the plurality of experience, 'Nature Morte' suggests that disturbance is inescapable even in the most controlled of domestic environments. *Poems* is a significant volume for both MacNeice's career and the literary history of the 1930s because of its tense amalgam of conflicting impulses, its refusal to resolve the tensions it identifies between individual and collective aspirations. Though 'Nature Morte' might seem remote from such debates, its sense of the perviousness of the 'solid and staid' to 'unrest' underlines the fragility of the lives it evokes. In this way, it prefigures the opening section of *Autumn Journal*, where MacNeice conflates the end of summer in 1938 with the slow 'Ebbing away' of 'the abandoned order' of middle-class southern England (*CP* 101–2).

This analysis suggests that as early as 1935, MacNeice's work was conceptually distinct from Spender and Day Lewis's. How then should we understand the affiliations within what Longley playfully describes as the 'MacNeice group'? I have argued that MacNeice and his colleagues respond to the influence of Eliot and Auden, reconceptualizing poetry as an implicitly political art form. For Day Lewis and Spender, this meant attempting to reconcile a contemporary poetic practice with a progressive political ideology. For MacNeice, this meant a poetic which drew its energies from the language and preoccupations of ordinary people. The poetry the three men produced during the early 1930s continuously points to the encroachment of the political and the public on the traditionally private domain of lyric poetry. Though they have been labelled as, following Spender's poem, 'pylon' poets – a group of technological neophytes who saw the electrification of Britain as a metaphor for its political transformation – the poetic evidence suggests that there were resistances and hesitancies in their attitude to the 'evil time' of the mid-1930s. All three wrote poetry where the private competes with the public; Spender's *Vienna* exemplifies the unsuccessful attempt to write a politically engaged poetry which is also revelatory of the poet's personal preoccupations. MacNeice's *Poems* reveal a more flexible interplay between poet and world.

Thus the miniature 'Aubade' (*CP* 28) stresses that the outside world increasingly impinges on escapist individualism. Answering the question 'What have we [...] to look forward to?', the poem concludes 'Not the twilight of the gods, but a precise dawn/ Of sallow and grey bricks, and newsboys crying war'. 'Twilight of the Gods' (*CP* 649) was the final poem in *Blind Fireworks*, an exuberant display of literary panache in which the dying Pythagoras conceives of the end of the world as a blizzard of 'The snowflakes of Nirvana [...]/ Covering this and that and the other thing'. For all the promise of its title, the poem ends 'in an impasse' where the described catastrophe has no clear symbolic relation to the world of the reader.[37] By revisiting this text, 'Aubade' economically dismisses MacNeice's juvenilia and underlines the new contexts in which the poet was working. In place of the vague apocalypse of the earlier poem, 'Aubade' anticipates 'a precise dawn' in a tangible world. This sense of the pressure of external events on poetry is shared by all three poets. Yet it is only in the work of the anti-conformist MacNeice that this tension is unequivocally turned to poetic advantage.

59

3

A Grain of Salt: The Later 1930s

The previous chapter argues that though there were subtle differences of political emphasis between MacNeice, Day Lewis and Spender, their writing of the early 1930s responds to analogous pressures. With *Poems*, MacNeice begins to define his own artistic agenda and to differentiate his work from that of his contemporaries. The volume's concern with the tensions between the individual and the group and within the routine and the mundane anticipates the lighter poetry of the late 1930s. In this work, the compromise between the ambition to 'make it new' and the ideal of a democratic poetic practice is at its clearest. This chapter investigates the intellectual and political backgrounds to MacNeice's lighter work through Auden's pioneering redefinition of lightness. By considering MacNeice's response to this, I stress his emerging independence from even the most pre-eminent of his contemporaries. While *Letters from Iceland* and *I Crossed the Minch* show MacNeice gathering strength from Auden's example, *Autumn Journal* demonstrates this new poetic at its furthest reach, juxtaposing the public with the private to communicate the manifold crises of 1938.

In the second half of the decade, the Spanish Civil War (1936–9) between the democratically elected Popular Front government and Franco's right-wing nationalist rebels came to embody the broader ideological struggle between progressive and reactionary forces. Hynes suggests that for the British literary left, the war was initially seen as 'the first battle in the apocalyptic struggle of Left and Right' in which 'Good was striking back at Evil'.[1] Auden's notorious 'Spain' preserves the vestiges of such optimism. Yet Spain quickly became symbolic of disappointment and disaffection. Reflecting on a holiday visit in 1936 in the bleaker context of 1938, MacNeice wrote that he left 'not realising/ That Spain would soon denote/ Our grief, our aspirations' (*CP* 114). The volumes Day Lewis and Spender published in 1938 and 1939 record their declining confidence in communism and the outcome of the war in Spain. Day Lewis's *Overtures to Death* is frankly pessimistic from its title onwards. War is conceived of as an inevitable pseudo-sexual climax: bombers' 'wombs [...] ache to be rid of death'. Conversely, phallic 'big guns [...] plant death in your world's soft womb': the German airstrikes which have destroyed Spanish cities 'will grow nearer home' (*CPDL* 269, 270). Though the long narrative poem 'The Nabarra' celebrates the 'Men of the Basque country, the Mar Cantabrico', who valiantly encountered a German destroyer in a sea battle, even this celebration is overcast by subsequent events. Day Lewis juxtaposes the Spanish fighters, for whom 'freedom was flesh and blood', with British advocates of appeasement, who 'gave up that country to rack and carnage'. The poem closes with the consolation of traditional poetic rhetoric, reminiscent of Shelley's *Adonais*, that the 'light' of the fighters 'still flashes like a star's that has turned to ashes', yet it is the undeceived sense that the 'Men of the basque country' have been sold out through 'the base coinage/ Of politicians' which gives the poem its pessimistic grandeur (*CPDL* 301–2).[2]

MacNeice was also clear that the conflict between Franco's rebels and the Spanish government engaged fundamental political issues – he unequivocally supported the *Left Review*'s campaign on behalf of the government (*Prose*, 42). Yet because he had never subscribed to communism, he had no need to update his ideological position: the edgy marriage of individualism with progressive idealism persists throughout his work of the later 1930s. *I Crossed the Minch* observes that 'A world society must be a federation of differentiated communities, not a long line of robots doing the goose-step' (*ICM* 12). While MacNeice ostensibly defends individualism, more interesting is the fact that the aspiration for a 'world society' remains credible. His publications of this period are amongst the most radical of his career both in terms of the political views which they espouse and in the lighter literary forms which they develop.

SERIOUS LIGHT VERSE

MacNeice's interest in lighter poetry partly derives from his collaboration with Auden. Auden had experimented with lighter forms from the late 1920s onwards. *Poems* and *The Orators* contain satiric parodies, though the recondite allusions in texts like 'Get there if you can' mean that, despite their formal levity, they remain challenging and opaque.[3] As Auden moved away from the obscurity of his first volumes, so he became conscious that lighter verse could be a conduit between poet and reader. *The Oxford Book of Light Verse* radically rereads English literary history to challenge the hegemony of 'difficult' poetry. Lightness is a component of all poetry which was siphoned out of the literary mainstream as a result of the Industrial Revolution and the consequent split between poets and their readers. Auden argues that the conventional understanding of light verse derives from this split by segregating poetry into the opposed camps of 'highbrow' art or 'trivial' social entertainment of *'vers de société*, triolets, smoke-room limericks'. Crucially, 'Light verse can be serious'; the category comprises a much broader conspectus of forms for Auden than it had for his Victorian and Edwardian predecessors.[4] MacNeice's review praises Auden for including 'comparatively little' *'vers de société'* in favour of 'nursery rhymes, broadsheets, folk ballads', arguing that such 'popular verse' displays a more 'genuine feeling or naturally felt attitude to life' (*SLC* 99). MacNeice underlines the radicalism of Auden's anthology: *The Oxford Book of Light Verse* incarnates a communicative poetics, which places the demotic alongside the canonical, and where the projected movement of poetry back towards its readers mirrors an ideal political levelling: 'poetry which is at the same time light and adult can only be written in a society which is both integrated and free'.[5]

This raises the question of whether MacNeice's lighter work simply shows him following Auden's lead. *Modern Poetry* certainly exhibits MacNeice's proximity to Auden. Since one of the book's central claims is that the poet is 'a specialist in something which every one practises', as a blend of 'trivial talk, humorous talk, joke-talk', lighter poetry challenges Matthew Arnold's conception of poetry as an art of 'high seriousness' (*MP*

178). Mirroring his plea for an *'impure* poetry', MacNeice insists that 'poetry can show every kind of blend of lightness and seriousness' (*MP* v, 178–9). Like ordinary speech, poetry is complicated and enriched by its polyvalent tonal compromises; there is no such thing as a poem which is purely serious or purely light. For Auden and MacNeice alike, lightness was an integral part of traditional poetry, a register closer to the everyday language of ordinary people than that of the poetry of 'high seriousness'.

Yet it would be misleading to read MacNeice's lighter work as a tributary development to Auden's. MacNeice's criticism shows a mixture of collegial support with sharper commentary: he praises 'Letter to Lord Byron' as a pastiche of Byron and a long poem 'of serious criticism in the lighter manner'; on the other hand, 'Miss Gee' is 'a piece of rather cruel spinster-baiting' (*MP* 188, 191). MacNeice's dislike of 'Miss Gee' exemplifies his dissent from the misogynistic consensus of his homosexual colleagues. 'Letter to W. H. Auden' (published in the Auden Double Number of *New Verse* of November 1937) amplifies his unease with Auden's 'present use of the ballad form':

> I hope that you will not start writing down to the crowd for, if you write down far enough, you will have to be careful to give them nothing that they don't know already and then your own end will be defeated. Compromise is necessary here, as always, in poetry. I think you have shown great sense in not writing 'proletarian' stuff [...] You realize that one must write about what one knows. One may not hold the bourgeois creed, but if one knows only bourgeois one must write about them. (*SLC* 85)

The 'Letter' touches on debates about whether the writer should 'go over' to the Proletariat and write from the perspective of the working class.[6] MacNeice's advice is emphatic: Auden should stick to writing about his own class and avoid patronizing his readers. Though 'Miss Gee' is very much a poem of distressed bourgeois life – its impoverished subject lives 'In a small bed-sitting room [...] On one hundred pounds a year' – MacNeice's point is that the ballad form lends itself to oversimplification. 'Miss Gee' resolves into the crude (though characteristically Audenesque) moral that sexual repression leads to cancer as an 'outlet' for the spinster's 'foiled creative fire'.[7] By insisting, in a way reminiscent of Spender's 'Poetry and Revolution', that the bourgeois writer must write about bourgeois subjects, the 'Letter' resists the progressive optimism which would inform *The Oxford Book of Light Verse*. Lightness does not inevitably lead to a socially inclusive poetry.

At issue here are literary tactics rather than political affiliations: writing about the bourgeoisie does not betoken acceptance of 'the bourgeois creed'. MacNeice has been easy to misrepresent because he avoided unambiguous statements of political intent. If 'Literary criticism's great vice is that it will take any individual poet as a pure specimen of any one tendency or attitude', it is unsurprising that literary history has been unable to accommodate MacNeice's deliberately pluralistic outlook (*MP* 78). The key term in his 1930s criticism is the unglamorous 'compromise' through which he conveys 'the manysidedness of poetry' as well as scepticism about 'writing down to the crowd' (*SLC* 99). Lightness was a potentially fertile area for poetic compromise: 'Many of the finest works of art are a conscious or (more often) unconscious compromise, the outcome of a dialectic of opposites – heroics tinctured with the grain of salt or satire leavened with sympathy' (*SLC* 100). Though such 'compromise' is congruent with Auden's model of poetry as communication, it does not ape Auden's theory. Since MacNeice did not adopt Auden's dialectical account of literary history, his account of lightness is more nuanced than Auden's. As he was sceptical of progressive political optimism, so he resisted progressive literary history. This difference of perspective informs their lighter work. Though *The Oxford Book of Light Verse* privileges popular ballads at the expense of *vers de société*, Auden was, as *Modern Poetry* recognized, a skilled parodist fluent in a range of traditional light verse forms.[8] As a poet, MacNeice is much more interested in what he calls the 'grain of salt' than in formal dexterity. His lighter work remains closer to what he calls 'Criticism of Life' rather than 'Escape' (*MP* 179). Between 1937 and 1938, Auden and MacNeice collaborated both on *Letters from Iceland* and in the articulation of a defence of lightness. But where Auden's historical determinism temporarily disguised his interest in the possibilities inherent within traditional forms, MacNeice's theory of compromise points to the complex mediation between the demands of art and concession to the expectations of readers.

Though *Autumn Journal* is acknowledged as one of the decade's most important poems, *Letters from Iceland* and *I Crossed the Minch* have struggled to find a critical audience. This has been for a number of reasons. *Letters from Iceland*'s status as a collaboration has told against it; from its first publication there has been uncertainty about who wrote what.[9] The poets' working relationship is usually configured in hierarchical terms, with Auden as the dominant partner; in consequence, MacNeice's contributions have been overlooked.[10] That both *Letters from Iceland* and *I Crossed the Minch* were avowedly written as potboilers has also made them problematic. If MacNeice was so contemptuous of his work that he could admit that his readers 'won't care if I know the history [of Lewis] or not', critics have not been disposed to disagree with him (*ICM* 206). Yet the compromised motives behind the texts mirror MacNeice's 'impure' poetics and the circumstances he was seeking to represent. To an extent, this makes for texts riven by, rather than founded on, compromise. Nevertheless, the interest of poems like 'Letter to Graham and Anna' and 'Bagpipe Music' lies in the tension they evoke between conflicting ambitions and imperatives as they seek simultaneously to divert the reader while conveying the pressures of the moment of writing.

'THE STUDENT OF PROSE AND CONDUCT': MacNEICE IN *LETTERS FROM ICELAND*

Though critics have minimized MacNeice's presence in *Letters from Iceland*, his image regularly punctuates the text. Auden photographed him five times: his features would have been more familiar to the first readers of the volume than Auden's own.[11] Facing page 32, part of 'Letter to Graham and Anna', an unshaven, out of focus MacNeice leers blearily towards his public. He wears the same cap seen in the frontispiece, jauntily smokes a cigarette and seems to be posed in the mouth of a tent; the photo is labelled 'The Student of Prose and Conduct', a line from Auden's 'Journey to Iceland' which gently twits the touristic ambition to see the sights of historic Iceland (*LI* 25). MacNeice was certainly a student of Auden's poetry, and these irreverent, democratizing photographs are an insistent reminder of his creative participation in the volume as a whole.[12]

MacNeice's poetic contributions to *Letters from Iceland*, 'Letter to Graham and Anna', 'Eclogue from Iceland', 'Iceland' and 'Epilogue' can be read as a suite reflecting on contemporary politics and the position of the poet, in which lighter idioms combine with travelogue. 'Letter to Graham and Anna' debates the ethics of the trip to Iceland in the context of impending European war. It explores the tension between escapism and commitment familiar from *Poems*, though in this case MacNeice asks the troubling questions of himself rather than a persona:

> But what am I doing here? Qu'allais-je faire
> Among these volcanic rocks and this grey air?
> Why go north when Cyprus and Madeira
> De jure if not de facto are much nearer?

(LI 31)

The lighter idiom is immediately apparent. Pararhymes like 'Madeira' and 'nearer' proliferate; at first the poem seems to mimic the comic effects of 'Letter for Lord Byron', as in the couplet 'The tourist sights have nothing like Stonehenge,/ The literature is all about revenge' (*LI* 32). Like 'Letter to Lord Byron', the 'Letter' is written in a hybrid style, amalgamating the comic with the self-consciously literary. MacNeice samples one of his favourite tags from Molière alongside the Latin legal terminology of 'De jure and de facto'.[13] He teases the reader with snatches of other languages in a self-consciously vulgar parody of the collage technique of *The Waste Land* and, especially, Pound's *Cantos*.[14] Unlike Pound, MacNeice translates his quotations, so that when the poem is at its most exhibitionist, quoting 'Aristotle's pedantic phraseology' in the original, the Greek is immediately glossed as 'found its nature' (*LI* 34). MacNeice may show off, but he does not want to lose sight of his readers. This points again to the 'impurity' of the 'Letter': despite its flippancy, the questions MacNeice demands of himself are serious, and provoke a more ruminative account of 'The obscure but powerful ethics of Going North' (*LI* 32). Aristotle's phrase gives a partial justification to the trip:

> We find our nature daily or try to find it,
> The old flame gutters, leaves red flames behind it.
> [...]

> In short we must keep moving to keep pace
> Or else drop into Limbo, the dead place.

MacNeice construes the journey north as a refuge from the European crisis: 'Here we can practise forgetfulness without/ A sense of guilt' (*LI* 34–5). Yet this is felt more as a convenient excuse which enables him to voice the anarchic impulse to escape than any wholly satisfactory resolution of the issues. Though the 'Letter' ends inconclusively, its fantasy of escape is exposed in the 'Eclogue from Iceland'. The ghost of Grettir Asmundson, a saga hero whose story MacNeice would later dramatise as *Grettir the Strong*, insists that both Ryan (MacNeice) and Craven (Auden) must 'Go back to where you belong' to make a 'Minute' gesture of defiance against the degradation of contemporary Europe: 'Hatred of hatred, assertion of human values,/ Which is now your only duty' (*LI* 134). Grettir's sombre advice reverberates in the 'Epilogue', addressed to Auden, where MacNeice rehearses the tension between escapism and political reality as he reviews 'our Iceland trip' from his Hampstead home (*LI* 259–61). The poem oscillates between celebration of the trip as a holiday from responsibility and the insistent sense of calamity, sometimes in the space of the same couplet: 'Time for the soul to stretch and spit/ Before the world comes back on it'. The trip was 'a fancy turn [...] Sandwiched in a graver show' of European upheaval:

> Down in Europe Seville fell,
> Nations germinating hell,
> The Olympic games were run –
> Spots upon the Aryan sun.

Though the text records the events of the summer of 1936 (the fall of Seville to Franco's forces, and the Berlin Olympics which Hitler designed as a demonstration of the supremacy of 'Aryan' races), and though MacNeice finds himself back in his English home, it fails to follow Grettir's advice. As the final poem in *Letters from Iceland*, it presents MacNeice trapped in a time and a place where even the 'Minute' heroic gestures Grettir had advocated seem impossible:

> Better were the northern skies
> Than this desert in disguise –
> Rugs and cushions and the long
> Mirror which repeats the song.

Like the paralysed bourgeois MacNeice had analysed in poems like 'Nature Morte', 'Epilogue' locates him in a 'desert in disguise', pessimistically waiting for 'The gun-butt raps upon the door' as 'Our prerogatives as men/ Will be cancelled' by some future dictatorship. The poet's own room 'becomes a pit'; as the future of Europe narrows, both London and his home become places of delusion and constriction. Conversely, 'Iceland' ruefully contrasts the poets' anxieties with the islanders' lifestyle:

> So we who have come
> As trippers North
> Have minds no match
> For this land's girth;
> The glacier's licking
> Tongues deride
> Our pride of life,
> Our flashy songs.
>
> But the people themselves
> Who live here
> Ignore the brooding
> Fear, the sphinx;
> And the radio
> With tags of tune
> Defies their pillared
> Basalt crags.

(LI 230)

Like 'Epilogue', 'Iceland' embodies MacNeice's distinctive adaptation of lighter idioms. In the tension between its playful technique and the graver import of its context, 'Iceland' exemplifies the model of lighter poetry as a grain of salt, directed towards both the poets' and the island's isolation. Internal rhyme is used both as a mocking jingle ('Tongues deride/ Our pride of life') and to undermine the islanders' ostensible tranquillity: the people 'Who live here/ Ignore the brooding/ Fear'. By slashing this last phrase across a line break, the poem graphically registers its omnipresence even in Iceland. Such touches confirm that this 'song' is purposefully 'flashy' as it uses the resources of poetry to dramatize the lack of symmetry between the poets and their environment. 'As trippers North' they 'Have minds no match/ For this land's girth': the

68

consciously flawed rhyme of 'North' with 'girth' underscores that difference.

MacNeice's deployment of unrhymed lines anticipates their similarly deflationary effect in *Autumn Journal*:

> And stocks go up and wrecks
> Are salved and politicians' reputations
> Go up like Jack-on-the-Beanstalk; only the Czechs
> Go down and without fighting.

(CP 119–20)

Though the rhyme of 'wrecks' with 'Czechs' leaves no doubt about the perfidy of the Munich Agreement (where the British prime minister Neville Chamberlain sold Czechoslovakia out to Hitler for the sake of prolonging peace), the sense of outrage is voiced by the bathetic downturn of 'Go down and without fighting'. Like 'Iceland', where 'the Sphinx' is left in spooky, unrhymed isolation, MacNeice exploits the reader's expectation of a fully rhymed close to deliver a more unsettling rebuke.

I CROSSED THE MINCH

The poems of *I Crossed the Minch* are more of a miscellany than those written for *Letters from Iceland*. That MacNeice's recycled seven poems from both travel books in *The Earth Compels* (amounting to twenty-five pages of a sixty-four-page volume) contributes to this impression. Yet *I Crossed the Minch* shows MacNeice successfully fusing levity with travel, while partially turning away from his own preoccupations. Even so, the travelogue recurs to familiar concerns. In the opening pages MacNeice mocks the 'sentimental and futile hope' that in going to the Hebrides he would reconnect with his Celtic origins, and celebrates his belonging to the 'clique' of 'wider civilisation' represented by an issue of the *Listener* full of work by and about his friends (*ICM* 3–4). The book repeatedly emphasizes its writer's cultural hybridity: he is simultaneously a tripper in search of his roots, a former public-school boy and a member of an English metropolitan elite. *I Crossed the Minch* is preoccupied by the ethics of travel writing. MacNeice presents himself as a dilettante, engaged in a literary chore he doesn't believe in, whose 'sympathies are Left', and yet whose prejudices remain rooted in the past: 'With my heart and my guts I lament the passing of class' (*ICM* 125, 27). Though these statements have been seen as further demonstrations of MacNeice's ingrained individualism, they come from a chapter entitled 'Dialogue with my Guardian Angel' which takes place 'On the island of Tiree, inside a tin shack' (*ICM* 123). The setting indicates that the chapter, like the book as a whole, is a performance. MacNeice plays himself as a yearning yet progressive snob, while the dialogue touches on ideas more seriously explored elsewhere. Though he admits that pure poetry would have no place 'In a city starving under siege', *Modern Poetry*'s model remains viable: 'Impure poetry of some sort will doubtless continue' (*ICM* 127).

I Crossed the Minch therefore embodies MacNeice's own theories. In particular, 'Life of Lord Leverhulme' and 'Bagpipe Music' administer a 'grain of salt' to the kinds of metropolitan attitudes MacNeice diagnoses in himself in the 'Dialogue'. Though the verse of 'Life of Lord Leverhulme' is designedly crude – it mimics the rambunctious directness of a bar-room ballad – it shows the adaptation of lightness for a satiric purpose.[15] MacNeice presents Lord Leverhulme (1851–1925), the soap manufacturer who 'patented the brand of Sunlight Soap', as a remorseless capitalist, whose credo forms the poem's refrain: 'Over the hills and across the skies,/ By God it pays to advertise' (*ICM* 79). The centre of the poem is the sardonic account of Lever's attempts to reorganize Lewis and Harris as enterprise economies. MacNeice's bitter vignette of Leverburgh (the fishing village Obbe renamed in Lever's honour in 1920) is emphatic:

> Leverburgh was meant to be
> The hub of the fishing industry;
> All that remained at Lever's death
> Was a waste of money and a waste of breath.
>
> All that remained of Lever's plans
> Were some half-built piers and some empty cans,
> And the islanders with no regrets
> Treated each other to cigarettes.
>
> (*ICM* 82)

The writing resonantly bears witness to the shortfall between Lever's grandiose plans and the reality of what he left. In

MacNeice's view, the casual exchange of cigarettes between islanders has a human value and integrity absent from Leverburgh's 'half-built piers'. The contrast between Lever's hubris and the undeceived attitudes of the islanders recurs throughout the latter stages of the poem. When St Peter interrogates the newly deceased Lever, 'Have you any failure to confess?', Lever admits 'The Western Islands had me beat'. Peter's response gets to the heart of *I Crossed the Minch*'s concern about the tension between the Gaelic-speaking islanders and English parochialism:

> The Scottish Islands are a rotten deal,
> Those Celts are terribly difficile;
> We find them unwilling to pull their weight
> When we let them in at the Golden Gate.
>
> They've no team spirit, they won't take part
> In our study circles and community art
> And at garden parties they won't concur
> In speaking English – which is *de rigueur*.

(ICM 83–4)

St Peter embodies the voice of metropolitan culture which MacNeice himself ventriloquizes elsewhere. But unlike Mac-Neice, who begins the book with the heartfelt regret 'I am very sorry that I know no Gaelic' (*ICM* 3), Peter negligently assumes the superiority of English while unconsciously speaking in the hybrid idiom of upper-class Franglais. Peter's speech is convincing class comedy ('Those Celts are terribly difficile') and positions the reader at an ironic distance from Lever's apparently philanthropic projects. The poem concludes with lines which exactly reflect how little Lever or the centralizing ambitions of English culture have affected the Hebrideans: 'far below in the Western Seas [...]/ The crofters gossiped in Gaelic speech/ And the waves crept over the lonely beach' (*ICM* 85).

Though the crofters have the last word in 'Life of Lord Leverhulme', 'Bagpipe Music' (*ICM* 159–60) conveys the economic and cultural decline of the Hebrides through an exhilarating nonsense poem. MacNeice described the poem as 'a satirical elegy for the Gaelic districts of Scotland and indeed for all traditional culture'.[16] It presents a series of comic vignettes of individuals struggling to survive in a changing environment:

The Laird o'Phelps spent Hogmanay declaring he was sober,
Counted his feet to prove the fact and found he had one foot over.
Mrs. Carmichael had her fifth, looked at the job with repulsion,
Said to the midwife, 'Take it away; I'm through with over-production'

(*ICM* 159–60)

This stanza juxtaposes people from different ends of Hebridean society, but, for each character, life has lost any sense of coherence. The laird insists on a sobriety he can't prove, while Mrs Carmichael turns away from her new child as an example of 'over-production' which neither she, nor by implication the islands, can sustain. In this context, the baby is a 'job', an economic rather than a human fact.

The poem fuses comic observation with a keen sense of the changes which were affecting Hebrideans: Willie Murray's brother catches 'three hundred cran when the seas were lavish', but finds that he earns more by going 'upon the parish' – that is, going on the dole – than by selling what he's caught. Similarly, the penultimate stanza brilliantly evokes the political scepticism of the islanders: 'It's no go the Government grants, it's no go the elections/ Sit on your arse for fifty years and hang your hat on a pension'. MacNeice unsentimentally offsets the rich texture of island life with a perception of impending economic and political catastrophe. The acuteness of the poem lies in its deft accommodation of credible vernacular tones ('Sit on your arse', 'Threw the bleeders back') with an undeceived sense of political reality: 'Work your hands from day to day, the winds will blow the profit'. The islanders have little chance of bettering their lot by work alone; the cosmopolitan paraphernalia of limousines, bank balances and even dance records they so energetically desire remain largely inaccessible: 'it's no go your culture'.

AUTUMN JOURNAL: NO MORE IDYLLS?

If *I Crossed the Minch* elegizes Hebridean culture from the perspective of a sympathetic outsider, *Autumn Journal* records an insider perspective on the immediate European crisis. The poem's tilting focus takes in places and institutions significant to MacNeice – Marlborough, Oxford, Birmingham, London – alongside broader views of the Europe of 1938. Spain occupies two entries; Ireland and Irish politics are excoriated in another. Czechoslovakia, and the imminent annexation of the Sudetenland by Nazi Germany, hovers beneath the first half of the poem as MacNeice restlessly considers the Munich agreement. Place, poetic form and political reality are intertwined throughout; following *Modern Poetry*, *Autumn Journal* refuses to separate literature from politics. It is an intensely self-conscious text, whose reflections on itself clarify MacNeice's intellectual agenda. Entry XVIII rejects traditional poetic forms as it registers the passing of traditional England:

> Sing us no more idylls, no more pastorals,
>   No more epics of the English earth;
> The country is a dwindling annexe to the factory,
>   Squalid as an after-birth.
>
> (CP 144)

The old forms have become blinds to the grim reality of industrial England, while the formulation that the country 'is a dwindling annexe to the factory' glances towards the more brutal annexations taking place in continental Europe. To underline the redundancy of the past, the entry articulates the fears of a society uncertain of its future and its values alike:

> Who knows if God, as Nietzsche said, is dead?
> There is straw to lay in the streets; call the hunchback,
>   The gentleman farmer, the village idiot, the Shropshire Lad,
> To insulate us if they can with coma
>   Before we all go mad.
>
> (CP 145)

Though MacNeice admired Housman, *A Shropshire Lad* becomes a shorthand for an outmoded poetry, rooted in traditions and social archetypes – gentlemen farmers, village idiots – whose day is past. Such poetry, like conservative fantasies of the vitality of tradition, has only a tranquillizing effect, delaying but not deferring what the entry later describes as 'The responsibility of moral choice' (CP 146). For *Autumn Journal*, poetry is coterminous with political and ethical judgements, though such judgements must not be confused with slogans. MacNeice described the poem as 'something half-way between the lyric and the didactic poem' (CP 791). As serious light verse, it is structured through such generic and tonal compromises.

73

Autumn Journal was one of MacNeice's most successful publications. After its first appearance in the spring of 1939, it was reprinted five times in the 1940s and three more times after that.[17] This success goes some way towards showing that MacNeice achieved his goal of writing poetry accessible and attractive to a broad reading public. Critics have largely endorsed this popular verdict, recognizing the poem as one of MacNeice's major works and as characteristic of its period; in Longley's formula, *Autumn Journal* 'synthesizes the loose ends of the 1930s into a personal and communal psychodrama'.[18] Nevertheless, the poem's form and orientation remain contentious. While some see the poem as formally loose, others feel that it is more carefully designed. McKinnon, though conscious of the organization within entries, saw no overall cohesion; conversely, McDonald argues that '*Autumn Journal* is conceived as inherently unstable'.[19] The debate about form usually overlaps with the reading of its political orientation. In one of the most influential discussions, Hynes views it as 'a passive poem', which voices the times rather than any individual perspective. This sense of the poem's passivity connects with Hynes's broader characterization of MacNeice as 'a charming Irish Classicist with upper-class tastes and a gift for making melancholy poems'.[20] By implication, such a poet would be congenitally unable to write a poem of active commitment. Hynes's view has been challenged by both Longley and McDonald; for Longley, *Autumn Journal* 'formulates an emotional, social, political and "ethical" response' to the Munich crisis.[21] At issue here is the value of the poem: is it, as MacNeice later implied, a predominantly journalistic text which documents the anxieties of 1938,[22] or can it be seen to have broader ambitions and claims on the reader's attention?

Form is crucial to *Autumn Journal*, but the subtlety of that form has only been appreciated intermittently. The title stresses the text's provisional cast; as MacNeice's Note explains, 'In a journal or a personal letter a man writes what he feels at the moment; to attempt scientific truthfulness would be – paradoxically – dishonest' (*CP* 791). Most critics recognize the honesty of *Autumn Journal*, even if they do not applaud its effect.[23] MacNeice's valorization of honesty is certainly at odds with Hynes's caricature of him as a melancholy aesthete. Moreover, the Note's apologetic tone – it begins by acknowledging the poem's personal and political 'over-statements' – disguises the fact that the choice of the journal form was neither arbitrary nor frivolous. By aligning journals with letters, MacNeice implicitly signals that *Autumn Journal* responds to 'Letter to Lord Byron'.

As we have seen, MacNeice was hugely impressed by the 'Letter'. *Modern Poetry* describes it as 'a *tour de force*, a challenge to the common statement that to adopt an earlier poet's manner leads merely to *pastiche*' (*MP* 189). If the 'Letter' is more than a pastiche of *Don Juan*, so *Autumn Journal* echoes Auden's poem without replicating its effects. The connections and divergences between the two poems underline the complex interrelations between Auden and MacNeice at this period. Despite its progressive political agenda, and its submerged gestures towards Auden's homosexuality,[24] the 'Letter' remains an updated form of traditional light verse, in which the poem's momentum derives from the outrageous ingenuity of its rhymes. As Auden's 'major exercise in comic verse', the 'Letter' is an exhibitionist display, which draws attention to its own rhyming procedures.[25] It is studded with pararhymes and bilingual rhymes – 'I'd caught a heavy cold in Akureyri,/ And lunch was late and life looked very dreary' (*LI* 19) – alongside rhymes which bathetically stress the subservience of meaning to the dictatorship of sound:

> Though it's in keeping with the best traditions
> For Travel Books to wander from the point
> (There is no other rhyme except anoint)

(LI 23)

The delight of the 'Letter' lies partly in the comic knowingness of its rhyming strategies. The failure to find another rhyme for 'point' other than the brazenly inapposite 'anoint' indicates the constraint which underlies all rhyming verse as well as Auden's self-confidence that he can capitalize on this failure. Similar provisionality and happenstance are built into the form of the 'Letter'. Though critics often forget that the poem was originally designed as a part of *Letters from Iceland*, and that its five parts are interspersed through that text, the structure of the book is crucial to the poem. Each of the first four parts is interrupted rather than finished: 'this, my opening chapter, has to stop'; 'I

75

must interrupt my screed to you,/ For I've some other little jobs to do'; 'The clock is striking and it's time for lunch [...]/ We shall be travelling, as they call it, light;/ We shall be sleeping in a tent to-night' (*LI* 24, 59, 107). Through such intrusions, Auden stresses the social character of his poem – that it is a 'screed' taken up in odd moments – a letter to Byron which must compete with letters home and social visits as well as the other texts which form the contents of *Letters from Iceland*. The end of 'Letter to Graham and Anna' shows MacNeice learning these lessons through the comic agency of Auden himself:

> And here – but Wystan has butted in again
> To say we must go out in the frightful rain
> To see a man about a horse and so
> I shall have to stop.

> (LI 35)

None of these texts is precisely what it purports to be: they are not genuine letters any more than *Autumn Journal* is 'a genuine journal', yet this is precisely the point.[26] By mimicking the casual tone and interrupted composition of real letters, Auden and MacNeice artfully advertise the impurity of their poetics, conveying the sense that poetry is a contingent practice which must take its chances with camping trips and 'the orchestral background' of 'The news from Europe' (*LI* 226).

Despite emerging from the collaboration on *Letters from Iceland*, *Autumn Journal* is a very different 'poem of serious criticism in the lighter manner' from 'Letter to Lord Byron'. Though equally dependent on rhyme, MacNeice largely eschews Auden's comic method in favour of what he called 'an elastic kind of quatrain',[27] typically rhyming ABCB or ABAC, where the A-rhymes tend to be single syllables and the unrhymed B and C words disyllabic. As we have seen, this can have the effect of throwing unrhymed words into relief –

> Who has left a scent on my life and left my walls
> Dancing over and over with her shadow,
> Whose hair is twined in all my waterfalls
> And all of London littered with remembered kisses.

> (CP 107)

– in which it is the clench of 'her shadow' with 'remembered kisses' which produces the climax. Occasionally, MacNeice uses polysyllabic rhymes in a way reminiscent of Auden:

> Aristotle was better who watched the insect breed,
>   The natural world develop,
> Stressing the function, scrapping the Form in Itself,
>   Taking the horse from the shelf and letting it gallop.
>
> (CP 129)

The rhyme imitates the virtues ascribed to Aristotle: as he was concerned with 'the function' of 'The natural world' (in opposition to Plato's ideal Forms) so the rhyme of 'develop' with 'gallop' moves from abstraction to the particular example of a horse in motion. The comic rhyme underscores important aspects of *Autumn Journal*: a critical concern with Classical education; the conversational 'thinking aloud' through a range of philosophical and ethical questions in a concrete idiom. Yet, unlike in Auden's poem, the vagaries of rhyme do not become an integral part of the poem's meaning; in consequence, *Autumn Journal* is less arch, less camp, than 'Letter to Lord Byron'.[28] Because it encompasses a range of tonalities, MacNeice often uses rhyme in *Autumn Journal* as a lyrical pivot to bind lines and quatrains together:

> But oh, not now my love, but oh my friend,
>   Can you not take it merely on trust that life is
> The only thing worth living and that dying
>   Had better be left to take care of itself in the end?
> For to have been born is in itself a triumph
>   Among all that waste of sperm
> And it is gratitude to wait the proper term
>   Or, if not gratitude, duty.
>
> (CP 154)

The rhyme scheme mutates from ABCA to ABBC as the speaker urgently seeks to persuade its addressee against the suicidal 'wish to quit'. Rhyme attempts to make the lines cohere as syntax and rhythm threaten to slip the knot. The elastic of the quatrain stretches almost to breaking point as the fourth line finds the rhyme 'in the end', but only after a dangerously slow accumulation of syllables. As MacNeice acknowledges immediately after this passage, 'I know you think these phrases high falutin': the artistic challenge of *Autumn Journal* was to effect a compromise between didacticism and lyricism, to make a poem simultaneously memorable and conversational. As this entry demonstrates, the tension was not always easy to manage. Nevertheless, what I have called MacNeice's thinking aloud remains crucial to the poem as a whole. Entries like this have been labelled as philosophical and as unsuccessful, yet as McDonald points out, MacNeice's 'philosophizing, *if it is that*, is drawn from vividly concrete bases'.[29] McDonald is right to be wary of the philosophical label. Whether MacNeice is comparing Aristotle and Plato or counselling against suicide, *Autumn Journal* is best understood as a form of poetic conversation, in which the speaker offers consciously provisional conclusions. Rhyme embodies the 'concrete bases' of that thinking. In this case, the lecture against suicide – 'it is gratitude to wait the proper term' – is chancily coupled with the ejaculation of 'all that waste of sperm'. Even as he preaches, MacNeice grounds his advice in the reality of sex and not just abstract nouns. It is the fertile 'sperm' which gets the lift of the rhyme with 'term' – a coupling which mimics the sexual exchange and points to the limitations on human life – rather than the sterile 'duty'.

If the rhyming of *Autumn Journal* shows MacNeice varying lessons he had learned from Auden, the journal form can also be seen as a refinement on the epistolary structure of 'Letter to Lord Byron'. Yet the Note's insistence on poetic honesty has had the effect of implying that the poem is an unmediated autobiographical record of MacNeice's opinions. His earlier summary of the poem, attached to a letter to Eliot of 22 November 1938, provides a more nuanced account of its method:

> Not strictly a journal but giving the tenor of my intellectual and emotional responses during that period. [...] It is written in sections averaging about 80 lines in length. This division gives it a *dramatic* quality, as different parts of myself (e.g. the anarchist, the defeatist, the sensual man, the philosopher, the would-be good citizen) can be given their say in turn.[30]

This formulation foregrounds the poem's '*dramatic* quality'. The letter does not so much conflict with the Note's assertion of honesty as modify its intensity: the poem gives the 'tenor' of MacNeice's 'intellectual and emotional responses' at a given point of time. As it could be said that the 'Letter to Lord Byron' is not strictly a letter, so *Autumn Journal* is 'Not strictly a journal'. The MacNeice who emerges through the poem is a representative individual, whose different and contradictory selves articulate impulses common to anyone of his age and class.

Autumn Journal is structured through a principle of dramatic intercutting. Successive entries juxtapose different attitudes and selves; ethical stances are improvised and modified through the course of the poem and in response to the pressure of events. To illustrate this principle, consider entries III to V, which progress from the end of the August bank holiday, the start of September and the outbreak of the Munich crisis. Though ostensibly concerned with different subjects, these entries powerfully convey the ties between the personal and the political. Unlike Spender's *Vienna*, the liaison between the two is unambiguous. Where III concludes in the voice of the 'would-be good citizen' with the inclusive aspiration to 'walk with the others' – the same people who had earlier been dismissed as 'accepters, born and bred to harness' – IV begins with a celebration of people in general: 'Nothing whatever can take/ The people away, there will always be people/ For friends or for lovers' (*CP* 107–9). The entry develops into one of MacNeice's most rapturous love lyrics, yet it remains rooted in the political concerns of the previous entry, initially embracing an erotic utopianism:

> [...] perhaps
> The conditions of love will be changed and its vices diminished
> And affection not lapse
> To narrow possessiveness, jealousy founded on vanity.

Following the previous entry's tentative commitment to progressive politics, here MacNeice reimagines love in almost prelapsarian terms. Nancy Sharp, the subject of this entry, is seen through the filter of this idealism, as it implicitly details the 'lapses' in their relationship. Although the poem registers the end of the relationship, the impulses to elegize and reproach are harnessed to a broader 'reckoning' which pays tribute to Nancy in terms which are not simply sensual or romantic:

> And it is on the strength of knowing you
> I reckon generous feeling more important
> Than the mere deliberating what to do

> When neither the pros nor cons affect the pulses.
> And though I have suffered from your special strength
> Who never flatter for points nor fake responses,
> I should be proud if I could evolve at length
> An equal thrust and pattern.

Entry IV shows the process of intercutting at its most dynamic. The reflections of MacNeice as the 'sensual man' who 'Inopportunely desired' Nancy 'On boats, on trains, on roads when walking' coexist with this more dispassionate tallying of her virtues. In turn, this admiration of her 'generous feeling' contributes to the poem's broader didactic agenda. Yet, crucially, this praise offers a contingent, particularized account of moral virtue, focused on Nancy, rather than any dogmatic credo. As 'Ode' had insisted 'I cannot draw up any code/ There are too many qualifications', so *Autumn Journal*'s structure resists evaluative stasis (*CP* 37). The journal form forces the reader to view MacNeice's moralizing as a form of ongoing improvisation, the terms of which must shift in response to the passage of time.

This necessarily fluctuating response to the times is vividly apparent in entry V as MacNeice documents the public anxieties of September 1938. Superficially, this shows the poem at its most journalistic, sampling news stories directly into the text: 'did you see/ The latest? You mean whether Cobb has bust the record [...]/ No, what we mean is Hodza, Henlein, Hitler,/ The Maginot Line' (*CP* 109–11). MacNeice juxtaposes John Cobb's failed attempt at the land speed record with the menacing names of the main protagonists in the Sudeten crisis (Henlein was the Sudeten German leader; Hodza was the Czech prime minister). In this context, the humane aspiration to 'evolve [...]/ An equal thrust and pattern' which closed the previous entry feels remote:

> To-day they were building in Oxford Street, the mortar
> Pleasant to smell,
> But now it seems futility, imbecility,
> To be building shops when nobody can tell
> What will happen next. What will happen
> We ask and waste the question on the air;
> Nelson is stone and Johnnie Walker moves his
> Legs like a cretin over Trafalgar Square.

In a way which is characteristic of the poem as a whole, these lines fuse sensitivity to the immediate in the smell of the mortar with an overarching sense of panic – deftly shown by the anaphoristic yet acutely conversational repetition 'What will happen' – alongside tense scepticism about the future. The senselessness of 'building shops' in these circumstances finds metaphoric expression in the literally petrified Nelson and the absurd commercial icon of the Johnnie Walker advert. Implicitly, the poem suggests that all Londoners are moving towards the future in a kind of alcoholic paralysis: 'we laugh it off and go round town in the evening/ And this, we say, is on me'. Though MacNeice was always alert to the social and individual pleasures of drinking, in this case it provides a metaphor which distils the atmosphere of political and moral crisis. The confidence of entries III and IV is effectually overturned by a sober reassessment of the recent past:

> And at this hour of the day it is no good saying
> 'Take away this cup';
> Having helped to fill it ourselves it is only logic
> That now we should drink it up.

Such sentiments might seem to endorse Hynes's reading of *Autumn Journal* as a passive poem: MacNeice aligns his community with Christ in the Garden of Gethsemane to suggest that it is far too late to change direction – 'we' must 'drink' the contents of the cup, however dangerous they may be. The quatrain recalls the end of entry III, which also ventriloquizes the New Testament:[31]

> None of our hearts are pure, we always have mixed motives,
> Are self deceivers, but the worst of all
> Deceits is to murmur 'Lord, I am not worthy'
> And, lying easy, turn your face to the wall.

(CP 106)

This passage plainly rebukes the passivity Hynes ascribed to the poem as a whole: becoming politically engaged is a moral imperative which cannot be avoided by the pretence of unworthiness. Two entries later, MacNeice's practical ethics have shifted to accommodate the communal upheaval of the Munich crisis. In each case, MacNeice subversively adopts biblical tags to voice the seductions of indifference or escapism.

81

There is nothing intrinsically passive about the 'logic' which leads to the claim 'we should drink it up'; if the formulation is weaker than its forerunner, this is because of the bleak contexts which underlie this entry. It is part of the strength of the journal form that it insists that all such moral evaluations are provisional, or, as a wartime poem would put it, 'evil and good/ Are relative to ourselves who are creatures of period' (*CP* 760).

Though most of entry V is concerned with the public emotions of September 1938, MacNeice illustrates the transition from complacency to crisis by intercutting back to his own life. He notices that his eiderdown, 'a wedding/ Present eight years back', has sprouted feathers:

> And the linen which I lie on came from Ireland
>> In the easy days
> When all I thought of was affection and comfort,
>> Petting and praise.

(CP 111)

Read in the manner of Hynes, such detail is little more than melancholy autobiographical colouring as the depressive poet nostalgically remembers a less troubled time. Yet such assessments drastically underestimate the formal sophistication of *Autumn Journal*, in which MacNeice as an individual – here in the guise of 'the defeatist' – eloquently registers the interplay between the personal and the public. 'In the easy days' of the early 1930s, he envisaged a life which was little more than 'Petting and praise': such matrimonial illusions mirror the wider complacency of society at large. These ideas are conveyed with a lightness of touch, a poignant immersion in the feel of the Irish linen, which embodies the paradox of serious light verse.

Remembering the passage from entry IV which describes 'the white/ Smoking stub your lips had touched with crimson' (*CP* 108), Philip Larkin noted that MacNeice 'displayed a sophisticated sentimentality about falling leaves and lipsticked cigarette stubs: he could have written the words of "These Foolish Things"'.[32] Larkin had a good ear for 'sophisticated sentimentality': 'An Arundel Tomb' concludes with the lightly MacNeicean sentiment that a medieval tomb could 'prove/ Our almost-instinct almost true:/ What will survive of us is love'.[33] A sophisticated sentimentality is one which recognizes the connections between the individual and the community, which refuses to rarefy or segregate poetic emotion from everyday emotion. *Autumn Journal's* many moments of nostalgia and reflection are sophisticated both by the luminous quality of description and by the moral urgency which underlies them. As entry V insists: 'the morning already/ Is with us, the day is to-day' (*CP* 111).

4

So What and What Matter? Poetry and Wartime

In December 1942, MacNeice wrote a poem which anticipates the end of 'our way of life', when the poets of his generation will be superseded by fascistic 'tight-lipped technocratic Conquistadores' (*CP* 231–2). 'Epitaph for Liberal Poets' registers cynical indifference to this prospect – 'And some shall say *So What* and some *What Matter,/* Ready under new names to exploit or be exploited' – alongside a recognition that liberalism was an illusion, that the poets themselves were more court jesters than what an earlier poem had called 'free lances' (*CP* 57): 'Who were expected – and paid – to be ourselves/ Conditioned to think freely'. 'Liberal' emphasizes the illusory quality of the poets' independence: they were never as radical or revolutionary as they assumed they were. However, the poem finally resists defeatism:

> Such silence then before us, pinned against the wall,
> Why need we whine? There is no way out, the birds
> Will tell us nothing more; we shall vanish first,
> Yet leave behind us certain frozen words
> Which some day, though not certainly, may melt
> And, for a moment or two, accentuate a thirst.

'Epitaph for Liberal Poets' stresses the improbability that art will survive long beyond its historical moment. Poets who 'whine[d]' during their lifetimes may leave behind 'certain frozen words': fame is a form of stasis with no guarantee that the deep-frozen texts 'may melt' into comprehensibility. At the height of the war in Europe, MacNeice critically reviews his classical education and his life of relative privilege: 'The Individual has died before; Catullus/ Went down young'. Catullus provides a point of comparison for the liberal poets themselves: 'Though our songs/ Were not so warm as his, our fate is no less cold'. MacNeicean fame was to become an increasingly chilly business. 'Memorandum to Horace' (1962) revisits Horace's boast that his poetry was a monument more lasting than bronze.[1] The poem asks why Horace troubles 'to be lapidary,/ Knowing posterity [...] neither will be able/ Let alone yours, to cope with language', anticipating a world of 'communicants in frozen sperm' who have outgrown linguistic communication (CP 603). MacNeice's glacial futures simultaneously convey scepticism about poetry's traditional claim to be a form of textual time travel alongside a stubborn predilection for the 'lapidary', syntactical and metrical forms of classical poetry. 'Epitaph for Liberal Poets' encapsulates this residual idealism: although the passage of time will reduce the poets' works to 'frozen words', the possibility that these fragmentary texts may 'for a moment or two, accentuate a thirst' remains imaginatively tenable. To accentuate a thirst is much less than to build a monument more lasting than bronze, yet it leaves a space for poetry to act as a potentially subversive stimulant.

Like the rest of the *Springboard* volume, 'Epitaph for Liberal Poets' is very much a text of its moment: a poem both of MacNeice's middle years – what another poem calls 'Mid-Passage' – and of the Second World War. Though *Autumn Journal* had sympathetically addressed 'the wish to quit, to make the great refusal' (CP 154), in the early 1940s the need to rebuke nihilism became imperative. The opening of *The Strings are False*, drafted in the early 1940s, anticipates 'Epitaph for Liberal Poets':

> So what? This modern equivalent of Pilate's 'What is truth?' comes often now to our lips and only too patly, we too being much of the time cynical and with as good reason as any old procurator, tired, bored with the details of Roman bureaucracy [...] a vista of desert studded to the horizon with pyramids of privilege apart from which there are only nomads who have little in their packs, next to nothing in their eyes. Thus here I am now on a boat going back to a war and my feelings are too mixt to disentangle. The passengers' faces are settled in gloom and I have plenty of reason to be gloomy too, being a mere nomad who has lost his tent. (SF 17)

Like the poem, the autobiography recognizes the allure of cynicism while emphasizing that it is too 'pat' a response.

Positioning himself as a modern 'nomad', returning on a crowded passenger boat from America to Europe in late 1940, MacNeice conflates the cynical indifference of 'So what' with the blasé knowingness of Pilate's 'What is truth?' Such cynicism masks the political realities of a modern world disturbingly similar to the ancient: 'pyramids of privilege' and penniless refugees are common to both; in such a context, 'mixt' feelings remain something of a luxury, an intellectual self-indulgence.

This chapter will 'disentangle' some of MacNeice's feelings through the evidence of his work during the 1940s. As 'Epitaph for Liberal Poets' implies, the war and the events which led up to it prompted all of these writers to reconsider their commitments. MacNeice has been seen as the least compromised by the upheavals of the late 1930s since he was never a communist, nor had been as publicly associated with progressive politics as Auden, Spender and Day Lewis. The careers of all of these writers have been read in terms of later documents such as Isherwood's *Christopher and his Kind*, which stages Auden and Isherwood's falling out of love with the progressive cause on the boat which took them to America in January 1939:

> One morning, when they were walking on the deck, Christopher heard himself say: 'You know, it just doesn't mean anything to me any more – the Popular Front, the party line, the anti-Fascist struggle. I suppose they're okay but something's wrong with me. I simply cannot swallow another mouthful.' To which Wystan answered: 'Neither can I.' Those were not their exact words, but, psychologically, it was as simple as that. They had been playing parts, repeating slogans created for them by others. Now they wanted to stop.[2]

In Isherwood's terms, 'the Popular Front, the party line, the anti-Fascist struggle' were 'slogans' which masked his real feelings – in his case, his nascent commitment to his homosexual identity. *Christopher and his Kind* creates a historical myth in which the enthusiasms of the 1930s are labelled as inauthentic, to be replaced by more valid preoccupations.

Though MacNeice spent most of 1940 in America and considered emigrating, his career does not altogether conform to a divide between the 1930s and beyond. 'Epitaph for Liberal Poets' is illuminating here: though it anticipates the end of a 'way of life' and a way of writing, it does not renounce progressive values even as it subjects them to ironic commentary. MacNeice's work of the early 1940s is in many ways a critical re-exploration and restatement of the preoccupations of both *Poems* and *Autumn Journal*. In 1941 he wrote, 'I am sorry to see so much self-flagellation, so many *Peccavis*, going on on the literary Left. We may not have done all that we could in the Thirties, but we did do something' (*SLC* 123–4). As *Autumn Journal* anticipated, the war demanded new responses from writers; unlike his contemporaries, MacNeice did not believe that it demanded he renounce his core beliefs, nor his emerging poetic. *The Strings are False* begins with a journey *back* to Europe whereas *Christopher and his Kind* ends with a journey *away* from Europe; these contrasting directions betoken real differences of allegiance. This chapter argues that MacNeice's work turns on three interrelated issues: his political allegiance and national identity; the moral and aesthetic question of how to respond to the war; and the critical re-examination of childhood experience. In all of these areas, MacNeice attempts to reply to the cynical reflex: so what?

WHAT A PLACE TO TALK OF WAR: QUESTIONS OF ALLEGIANCE

The Strings are False suggests that the war challenged MacNeice's commitment, especially in relation to national identity.[3] This has been the focus of much recent commentary: Longley and McDonald have emphasized the complexity of MacNeice's Irishness in response to commentators who viewed him as more of a writer of metropolitan London who happened to have Irish roots. Stressing the cultural links between MacNeice and Irish poetry, Longley argues 'MacNeice is the major Irish poet after Yeats who follows him in broad cultural orientation'.[4] Similarly, Paul Muldoon's *Faber Book of Contemporary Irish Poetry* places MacNeice at the head of post-Yeatsian Irish poetry alongside Patrick Kavanagh, with some sixty pages of poems from throughout his career.[5]

As this work has shown, MacNeice's writing about Ireland conveys intensely mixed feelings. 'Valediction' (1934) and *Autumn Journal* XVI (both included by Muldoon) repudiate competing myths of Irishness. In the former, the speaker promises to 'exorcise [his] blood', while the latter simmers with contempt for both sides in his own 'darkest Ulster': 'Up the Rebels, To Hell with the Pope,/ And God Save – as you prefer – the King or Ireland' (CP 9, 138). Though MacNeice supported Home Rule (following what he took to be his father's position; see SF 62, 71), he was dismayed by the conservatism of de Valera's government and repelled by its attempts to resurrect Gaelic culture: 'Let the school-children fumble their sums/ In a half-dead language;/ Let the censor be busy on books' (CP 139–40). These are consciously unstable texts which court emotional extremity both as a strategy of provocation and to underline the artificiality of ideas of national identity. Both reflect on the patriotic feminization of Ireland as a symbolic mother. Autumn Journal demands 'Why/ Must a country, like a ship or a car, be always female,/ Mother or sweetheart?', while 'Valediction' makes the pained self-assessment, 'Cursèd be he that curses his mother. I cannot be/ Anyone else than what this land engendered me' (CP 138, 8). As the loss of his own mother was emotionally inescapable, so the alternately hostile and nostalgic relationship between MacNeice and his country could not be unproblematically resolved.

During the 1940s, MacNeice's attitude towards Ireland becomes a barometer of his literary and political moods. In September 1939, he was holidaying in the west of Ireland while working on two complementary Irish projects: the monograph, *The Poetry of W. B. Yeats,* and the sequence which was first published as 'The Coming of War', later revised as 'The Closing Album'.[6] *The Poetry of W. B. Yeats* updates the thinking of 'Poetry To-day' and *Modern Poetry.* By exploring a poet whose work was diametrically opposed to the communicative poetics and progressive political commitments of the poets of the 1930s – and whom Day Lewis had failed to assimilate to his myth of literary ancestry – MacNeice works through some of the exaggerations of his earlier work.[7] Yet *The Poetry of W. B. Yeats* is not a recantation of *Modern Poetry.* MacNeice maintains his earlier proposition that the poet is closer to the ordinary man than the mystic and insists, in typically un-Yeatsian fashion, that poets need to have an intellectual agenda (PY 24). Although Yeats's aestheticism remains unpalatable to MacNeice, the opening of the book registers that the war drastically relativizes the differences between his generation and Yeats:

> I had only written a little of this book when Germany invaded Poland. On that day I was in Galway. As soon as I heard on the wireless of the outbreak of war, Galway became unreal. And Yeats and his poetry became unreal also. [...] My friends had been writing for years about guns and frontiers and factories, about the 'facts' of psychology, politics, science, economics, but the fact of war made their writing seem as remote as the pleasure dome in Xanadu. For war spares neither the poetry of Xanadu nor the poetry of pylons. I gradually inferred, as I recovered from the shock of war, that both these kinds of poetry stand or fall together. War does not prove that one is better or worse than the other; it attempts to disprove both. (PY 17–18)

The war overturns previously fashionable axioms: the poetry of 'guns and frontiers and factories' (represented as so often by Spender's 'The Pylons') becomes as artificial and as fragile as Coleridge's 'Kubla Khan'. As 'Epitaph for Liberal Poets' would imply, MacNeice posits a subcutaneous continuity of outlook between the classics and the poets of his generation.

This sense of the destructive unreality of war connects *The Poetry of W. B. Yeats* with 'The Coming of War'. The sequence explores the disparity between various places in Ireland and the European war. 'Galway', which recalls the opening paragraph of *The Poetry of W. B. Yeats*, juxtaposes a Yeatsian evocation of a Yeatsian milieu – 'The night was gay/ With the moon's music' – with the insistent refrain: 'The war came down on us here' (CP 181–2). Poems later dropped from the sequence record the speaker's impulse to run 'away from the War' alongside the recognition that 'no one/ Can drive the War away' (CP 683, 685). The juxtaposition of a largely peaceful Ireland with an ominous, unseen Europe is at its finest in 'Cushendun' (CP 180), an outwardly pastoral evocation of Cushendun Bay in County Antrim, where John MacNeice had taken a summer house:

> Forgetfulness: brass lamps and copper jugs
> And home-made bread and the smell of turf or flax
> And the air a glove and the water lathering easy
> And convolvulus in the hedge.

(CP 180)

89

The relaxed rhythms and gently accumulating phrases collude with the notion that 'Forgetfulness' is not necessarily culpable – that, seen generously, it is a necessary condition for holiday relaxation. But the poem's sensuous world of 'home-made bread' and 'water lathering easy' is interrupted by the final stanza which forces the reader to re-evaluate 'Forgetfulness':

> Only in the dark green room beside the fire
> With the curtains drawn against the winds and waves
> There is a little box with a well-bred voice:
> What a place to talk of War.

As Stallworthy observes, 'everything has been altered by the shocking revelation of the last word'.[8] The subtlety of 'Cushendun' lies in the pointed doubleness of that closure: 'What a place to talk of War' registers without embellishment the disparity between the beauties of the place and the grimness of the moment. Yet the sheer blandness of the line opens the darker ethical suggestion in 'Forgetfulness'. The previous fifteen lines mask the context, which flares in that final word: the speaker has been deliberately trying to forget what is revealed by the 'little box'. Moreover, the stanza's subtle distinction between the radio's audience and the voice it projects heightens the conflict. 'Cushendun' juxtaposes its Northern Irish setting with the 'well-bred voice' of BBC radio, an institution for which, ironically, MacNeice would shortly work. Talking of war is not only at odds with Cushendun as a place, the timbre of the voice itself is felt as an alien intrusion on that landscape.

'The Coming of War' shares the ambivalence of the opening chapter of *The Strings are False* as it recurs to the fantasy of escape. But even as the sequence praises parts of Ireland, it insists on MacNeice's status as an outsider: Dublin 'will not/ Have me alive or dead' (*CP* 179). Elsewhere, he runs away from 'the Black/ North – the winch and the windlass,/ The drum and the Union Jack': Ulster is no more plausible as a refuge than Dublin (*CP* 683). The sequence is very much a poem of transition: from the political uncertainties of the late 1930s, from the hostile representation of Ireland in texts like 'Valediction' and *Autumn Journal*, and from the poetic styles of the 1930s volumes. This transitional flavour is textually embodied in the fluctuating dimensions of the sequence from *The Last Ditch* to

Collected Poems 1925–1948: as the sequence shows a protagonist unable to make up his mind, so the text reveals a poet uncertain of his way forward artistically.

Yet, as *The Strings are False* indicates, MacNeice felt the war engaged fundamental issues of commitment. Though the Allied cause is only 'a Lesser Evil' which may lead only to the 'problematical betterment for most likely a mere minority in a dubious and dirty future', MacNeice's return to Britain committed him to the fight against fascism (*SF* 21). His engagement with the war did not undermine his sceptical belief in progressive ideals. At this time, his BBC work was explicitly propagandist: he wrote 'propaganda features, which [...] I thought necessary and which I did as well – and that also means as truthfully – as I could'.[9] In a feature produced for the BBC Forces programme in July 1942, MacNeice constructed a satirical psycho-biography of Hitler, characterizing him as 'the shame of the human species'.[10] As Heather Clark argues, MacNeice's 'BBC work was not a question of prostituting his talent, but rather of fighting fascism'.[11] Ireland's wartime neutrality conflicted with MacNeice's political convictions. This conflict underpins 'Neutrality' (1942). Though McDonald cautions that the poem conveys 'much less than the whole story about the poet's complicated feelings', it remains 'an emphatic and pained' rejection of Irish foreign policy:[12]

> The neutral island facing the Atlantic,
> The neutral island in the heart of man,
> Are bitterly soft reminders of the beginnings
> That ended before the end began.
> [...]
> But then look eastward from your heart, there bulks
> A continent, close, dark, as archetypal sin,
> While to the west off your own shores the mackerel
> Are fat – on the flesh of your kin.

(CP 224)

Unlike 'Valediction' and *Autumn Journal* XVI, 'Neutrality' is rhetorically distanced from MacNeice's own experience. Nevertheless, its poetic strategies demonstrate the 'bitter' issues at stake for the poet in this argument. Through the classical device of apostrophe, 'Neutrality' juxtaposes idealized images of Irish topography with the reality of the war in Europe and the

Atlantic. When you 'Look into your heart', you find the beauty of the Irish landscape and past – 'A Knocknarea with for navel a cairn of stones'; 'fermenting rivers,/ Intricacies of gloom and glint' – alongside the perfidy of the Irish present – 'to the west off your own shores the mackerel/ Are fat – on the flesh of your kin'. MacNeice is unequivocal: though his Irish friends had asked him what the war had to do with him, 'Neutrality' asserts the ties of kinship between the Irish and those dying in the Atlantic. In this view, there are no 'neutral' national origins or 'beginnings'. By stressing the 'archetypal sin' of fascism, the final stanza fatally compromises both the beauty which the poem had found in the Irish landscape and the politics of neutrality.

'Neutrality' is very much a poem of the Second World War, centring on Irish foreign policy and the way in which such policies inflect ideas of belonging. With the end of the war, MacNeice's attitude towards Ireland became less polemical. While working in Ireland on *The Dark Tower* between May and September 1945, he wrote a series of short poems whose Irish settings provoke meditations on loss and belonging.[13] As 'Carrick Revisited' explains, these are texts in which MacNeice finds himself 'dumbfounded to find myself/ In a topographical frame' (*CP* 261–2). They revisit the tourist album technique of 'The Coming of War' to reassess models of home and identity in the wake of that war.

Like the earlier sequence, many of these are autobiographical poems. 'The Strand' elegizes John MacNeice (who died in 1942) through the evocation of the Achill Island in the west of Ireland, the area from which the MacNeice family originated: 'My father [...] / So loved the western sea and no tree's green/ Fulfilled him like these contours of Slievemore' (*CP* 263–4). As for John MacNeice, the west of Ireland becomes an imaginative touchstone for his son in 'Western Landscape', which exuberantly 'honour[s] this country' in 'doggerel and stout' (*CP* 265). MacNeice places himself in a relationship to the west at once rhapsodic and distanced:

> Let now the visitor, although disfranchised
> In the constituencies of quartz and bog-oak
> And ousted from the elemental congress,
> Let me at least in token that my mother

Earth was a rocky earth with breasts uncovered
To suckle solitary intellects
And limber instincts, let me, if a bastard
Out of the West by urban civilization
(Which unwished father claims me – so I must take
What I can before I go) let me who am neither Brandan
Free of all roots nor yet a rooted peasant
Here add one stone to the indifferent cairn ...

(CP 267)

The helter-skelter free verse, its riding, unsettled syntax which mimics the movement of the sea and the blurred, shifting line between sea and land, points to the uncertain position of the speaker. The poem claims kinship with this landscape, whilst stressing that its speaker is a 'visitor' to the west, 'disfranchised' from its 'constituencies'. Though he evokes Brandan's legendary journeys from Dingle in a curragh, he recognizes that he is neither this saint 'Free of all roots' nor a 'rooted peasant'. He is the 'bastard' child of 'urban civilization' irretrievably separated from his 'mother/ Earth'. As this last phrase demonstrates, despite its appearance of freedom, the text is orchestrated to emphasize that apartness.

These poems of the mid-1940s do not fully revise the stark polarities of 'Neutrality' nor the disjunction between persona and environment which underlies 'The Coming of War'. Though warmer in their regard for the west, they refuse to sentimentalize Ireland even as they honour its disparate topographies. 'Slum Song' notes the poverty of contemporary Dublin alongside the shortfall between aspiration and actuality. The folksong-like refrain, 'Wander far and near', with its expansive sense of life as an adventure, is tethered to rhyming reportage which insists on the economic limitations to such fantasies: 'the grown man must play the horses [...]/ But the blacks will remain to draw the hearses' (HS 28).[14] In 'Carrick Revisited', MacNeice returns to Carrickfergus, not to rediscover his past, but to register its distance and occlusion: 'Our past we know/ But not its meaning – whether it meant well' (CP 261–2). Though 'Time and place' are 'our bridgeheads into reality', they are also its 'concealment'. MacNeice's childhood 'remains [...]/ Like a belated rock in the red Antrim clay' and is unalterable: 'what chance misspelt/ May never now be righted by my choice'. Like the Dublin slum dwellers, MacNeice is constructed by his past and unable to escape from it. To revisit is not necessarily to recant: the poem also remembers 'Carrickfergus', which describes preparations for the First World War as a way of anticipating the Second (*CP* 55–6).[15] 'Carrick Revisited' begins with the speaker confused about his historical placement as the two wars become fused: 'Back to Carrick, the castle as plumb assured/ As thirty years ago – Which war was which?' 'Carrickfergus' voices the anxiety that 'the war would last for ever'; 'Carrick Revisited' responds with the admission that 'the child's astonishment' is 'not yet cured'. While at one level, this is an astonishment at the unchanging appearance of Carrickfergus, it also points to the ways in which MacNeice's sense of self is irrevocably involved with these wars.

This conception of Ireland as a place in which myth abrades reality is at its sharpest in 'Last Before America', which evokes nineteenth-century mass emigrations from Ireland. McDonald contends that the poem partly 'revises the terms of "Neutrality" by suggesting that Ireland is not deliberately sealed off from its context'.[16] Certainly, 'Last Before America' is less polemical than 'Neutrality'. Nevertheless, its ambivalent reading of emigration must also be understood in terms of MacNeice's own experience during the 1940s. The first two stanzas juxtapose families on the point of departure with the nostalgia of emigrants for the old country: 'From the bourn of emigrant uncle and son, a defeated/ Music that yearns and abdicates' (*CP* 264). Though sympathetic to this nostalgia, the poem insists on the realities of emigration: 'The decree/ Of the sea's divorce is final'. The last two stanzas undermine fantasies of emigration while recognizing the hold of the myth of the good place on the imagination:

> Pennsylvania or Boston? It was another name,
> A land of a better because an impossible promise
> Which split these families; it was to be a journey
> Away from death — yet the travellers died the same
> As those who stayed in Ireland.

> Both myth and seismic history have been long suppressed
> Which made and unmade Hy Brasil – now an image
> For those who despise charts but find their dream's endorsement
> In certain long low islets snouting towards the west
> Like cubs that have lost their mother.

Like 'Western Landscape', 'Last Before America' ends with a complex mixture of realism and unpurged lyricism, facing both the real west of 'Pennsylvania or Boston' and the mythical 'Hy Brasil'. The penultimate stanza underlines what has been implicit in the first half of the poem: the 'impossible promise' of emigration cannot disguise the fact that 'the travellers died the same/ As those who stayed'. Yet the final stanza partially recovers the Atlantis-like island Hy Brasil as a metaphor for the attraction of myth. Though in the realist terms of the previous stanza, Hy Brasil is a fantasy, it remains for idealists – 'those who despise charts' – an endorsement of their dreams, another 'impossible promise' of emotional plenitude. The poem's difficulty is that while it endorses this fantasy through the evocative simile of the last two lines, the caveats and qualifications which shape this image insist that Hy Brasil is little more than a 'suppressed' dream, a ghost memory of a childhood fantasy like the earlier 'chimney-smoke and spindrift' of the emigrants' accordion music.

All of these Irish poems are texts of troubled revisiting. 'Last Before America' exemplifies MacNeice's complex sense of his own identity, fantasizing a return to the mythical west while remembering that 'The decree/ Of the sea's divorce is final'. As I have suggested, these poems handle complex issues of belonging and loss; the losses of the war years are never far from the surface. In 'Littoral', the imagistic description of a beach includes 'a widow/ Who knits for her sons but remembers a tomb in another land' (*CP* 259). 'Last Before America' avoids direct allusion to the war, yet in its insistence that emigrations shape identity it underlines what was at stake for MacNeice in his return to Britain. *Holes in the Sky*, moreover, places these 'Irish' poems in distinctively 'English' literary contexts. The pages which follow include 'The Cyclist', which evokes the white horses of the Marlborough Downs, and 'Woods', which juxtaposes John MacNeice's preference for the Irish landscape with Louis's intoxication with the English woods of Malory, Shakespeare, Keats and Herrick (*HS* 38–40). Shakespeare is a significant presence in 'Autolycus', which conflates 'the Master' dramatist with the conny-catching rogue of *The Winter's Tale* to assert a trans-historical continuum between the past and the present: 'why should we forgive you/ Did we not know that, though more self-reliant/ Than we, you too were born and grew up in a fix?'

(*CP* 274–5).[17] The overlapping terms of Irishness and Englishness are deeply embroiled in this 'fix'. Shakespeare – and by implication the English literary tradition – continues to matter not because he stands outside of time but because his work retains the confusion and the fixes of his historical moment.

LONGING TO BE COMBINED INTO A WORKING WHOLE: MacNEICE AT WAR

MacNeice's wartime poems are the most underrated part of his work. As Clark has demonstrated, the next generation of Northern Irish poets, Seamus Heaney, Michael Longley and Derek Mahon, downplayed his wartime work in favour of 'the lyric, nostalgic, and apolitical MacNeice'.[18] In consequence, the force of MacNeice's ideological commitment to the Allied war effort has been obscured. Stallworthy's condemnation of *Springboard* because its poems 'are much more public than private' is representative of this preference.[19] Yet this is precisely the effect which MacNeice was aiming for. His wartime poems aspire to the condition of public utterance, which can articulate the upheavals of the war and the struggle against fascism credibly and without patriotic inflation.

Despite the rhetoric of the 1930s, few of the poets successfully adopted a public voice: the controversy surrounding Auden's 'Spain' exemplifies the difficulties they faced in addressing public themes.[20] Day Lewis's 'Where are the War Poets?', from *Word Over All* (1943), voices the resistance left-leaning poets felt when called on 'to speak up in freedom's cause' (*CPDL* 335). The issue was who was doing the calling: for Day Lewis, producing verse at the behest of 'They who in folly or mere greed/ Enslaved religion, market, laws' compromises the act of writing. The war is 'No subject for immortal verse', and such work would only 'Defend the bad against the worse'. Although *The Strings are False* shows MacNeice sharing some of Day Lewis's misgivings, he was ultimately in no doubt that Nazi Germany was significantly 'worse' than democratic Britain, however 'bad' that might seem.

Out of such contexts, *Springboard* attempts to find a credible voice, or voices, of solidarity. The strength of these texts lies partly in their refusal to sloganeer. They are preoccupied with the difficulties of communication and of establishing agreement between people ostensibly on the same side. If 'Epitaph for Liberal Poets' insinuates that the politics of MacNeice's generation were a conditioned reflex, 'Babel'(CP 227–8) challenges its readers to rediscover a progressive consensus. The poem retells the biblical parable of the Tower of Babel (originally a warning against human aspiration to God-like power)[21] to question the feasibility of genuine communication between different groups:

Exiles all as we are in a foreign city,
    Can't we ever, my love, speak in the same language?
We cut each other's throats out of our great self-pity –
    Have we no aims in common?

(*CP* 227–8)

'Babel' is a poem about how we talk to one another. Through the counterpoint between the two refrain lines, MacNeice juxtaposes the language of lovers – 'Can't we ever, my love, speak in the same language?' – with a blander, more public idiom: 'Have we no aims in common?' Since wartime London becomes 'a foreign city' in which 'we' are 'Exiles all', these different idioms are potentially congruent. Yet the shortfall in communication is aurally emphasized by ruptures in the formal pattern: the refrains are of unequal metrical length and fail to rhyme with one another. That the poem establishes no symmetry between these questions intimates that the search for a common language may be in vain.[22] 'Babel' does not offer a blueprint for a better world. Rather, it challenges its cast of 'Patriots, dreamers, die-hards, theoreticians' (reminiscent of the passengers on the Atlantic crossing in *The Strings are False*) to face up to the alternatives to solidarity: cutting each other's throats or going 'to the wall'.

As 'Babel' addresses the disparate communities of a squabbling wartime city, other poems use particular individuals to illustrate broader social and intellectual trends. MacNeice's prefatory Note shows his awareness of the artistic risks he was taking:

Many of my titles in this book have the definite article, e.g. 'The Satirist', 'The Conscript'. The reader must not think that I am offering him a set of Theophrastean characters. I am not generalising; 'The

97

Conscript' does not stand for all conscripts but for an imagined individual; any such individual seems to me to have an absolute quality which the definite article recognizes. (*CP* 804)

The distinction between imagined individuals and generalized characters is an uneasy one which the poems do not always support. The reader is left in no doubt that 'The Conscript' is a symbolic individual who 'feels the weight of history/ Like clay around his boots' (*CP* 224–5). For the poem to work, the subject must reflect broader social realities – despite MacNeice's protestation, the conscript is a miniature emblem of the 'Choiceless' millions of young men conscripted during the war whose lives had 'no/ Promise but of diminishing returns'. 'The Conscript' reads more as an exercise in empathy than the thing in itself; it is artistically overdetermined in its anxiety to be both 'imagined' and 'absolute'. However, in the stronger poems, the focus on representative individuals, whether real or imagined, enables MacNeice to diagnose the psychology of the war.

Springboard sees the war largely from the perspective of the home front. MacNeice focuses not only on the Blitz, in 'Brother Fire' and 'The Trolls', but also on people who are often, as 'Bottleneck' puts it, 'non-combatant'. 'Swing-Song' filters bombing raids through the thoughts of 'a wartime working girl', imagining her young man in the thick of an RAF mission; 'The Mixer' describes a First World War veteran, a 'Colourless' clubbable man who has no way of coping with 'this second war which is fearful too' (*CP* 222–3, 226). MacNeice uses these uncertain personae as a way of refracting the experience of war, implying rather than stating the gravity of issues at play in the conflict. Thus 'Swing-Song' parodies the idiom of contemporary song, creating a tension between its glib surface and the situation it describes; the refrain conflates jazz rhythms with those of aerial bombardment: 'K for Kitty calling P for Prue .../ Bomb Doors Open .../ Over to You'.

The individuals of these poems grapple with the same kind of existential questions which troubled MacNeice. 'Bottleneck' considers the impasse between idealism and engagement as it focuses on a moral absolutist: 'Never to fight unless from a pure motive/ And for a clear end was his unwritten rule' (*CP* 223). Though exhibiting many of the impulses of MacNeice's generation, the poem distances the reader from the character by suggesting that his values are untested and poorly thought out. Through the 'progressive school' of 'books and visions', he has 'dreamt of barricades': his 'unwritten rules' derive from idealistic motives rather than any substantive contact with the outside world. MacNeice goes on to visualize a man in the throes of moral turmoil:

> When I saw him last, carving the longshore mist
> With an ascetic profile, he was standing
> Watching the troopship leave, he did not speak
> But from his eyes there peered a furtive footsore envy
> Of those who sailed away to make an opposed landing –
> So calm because so young, so lethal because so meek.

'Bottleneck' offers a biting critique of the protagonist's disengagement. He watches 'the troop ship leave' voyeuristically: his 'furtive footsore envy' of the young soldiers reflects his self-absorption and his inability to move beyond his 'ascetic', self-imposed values. The poem's diagnosis is that he will 'always be non-combatant/ Being too violent in soul to kill/ Anyone but himself' – he is another MacNeicean nihilist, unable to reconcile his ideals with the temptation to self-destruction. 'Bottleneck' rephrases the question of communal engagement and shared values. Though the protagonist is finally constrained by 'The permanent bottleneck of his highmindedness', his dilemma illuminates the need for 'compromise[s] with fact':

> in his mind
> A crowd of odd components mutter and press
> For compromise with fact, longing to be combined
> Into a working whole

This recalls imagery MacNeice had used to sketch a progressive society in 1935: 'Communism in the truer sense is an effort to think, and think into action, human society as an organism' (SLC 6). The 'longing to be combined/ Into a working whole' surfaces throughout Springboard, and underpins the rest of MacNeice's career. This is not to say that he realized this longing in ways which the persona of 'Bottleneck' could not, any more than it is to suggest that MacNeice was a communist in 1935. The point is rather that the aspiration towards some form of integration of the individual with society remained pivotal. As Caudwell continued to remind him, the 'paradox of art' is that 'man withdraw[s] from his fellows into the world of art, only to enter more closely into communion with humanity'.[23]

MacNeice's work as both poet and broadcaster during the 1940s refuses to segregate art from its audience. The title poem of *Springboard* is important in this respect as a diffident statement of faith and as an anticipation of the method of the parable poems of the later volumes. Like its companion poems, 'The Springboard' makes a strenuous compromise between the circumstances of the war and individual impulses. It imagines a diver 'High above London, naked in the night', who must 'dive like a bomber past the broken steeple' to wipe out 'his own original sin' and to save the people of London (*CP* 235–6). The diver is humanized by his fear of death and his reluctance to act the part of a hero: 'His blood began to haggle over the price/ History would pay if he were to throw himself down'. Though he is described as 'crucified among the budding stars', MacNeice stresses the diver's pragmatic 'unbelief'. In circumstances which 'called for sacrifice', the reader must configure his actions in flat, secular terms:

> If it would mend the world, that would be worth while
> But he, quite rightly, long had ceased to believe
> In any Utopia or in Peace-upon-Earth;
> His friends would find in his death neither ransom nor reprieve
> But only a grain of faith – for what it was worth.

These lines translate the diver's sacrifice into ordinary language: the reader is denied the rhetorical inflation of 'Peace-upon-Earth' in place of a conspicuously prosy and truistic language: 'quite rightly'; 'for what it was worth'. Such linguistic manoeuvres are characteristic of MacNeice's later work, which finds poetic strength in conversational idioms even as it works to estrange that language from its originating contexts. In 'The Springboard', while demotic phraseology keeps the diver's sacrifice tangible, it also disguises the surreal and parabolic quality of the poem as a whole. Like George Herbert, MacNeice excels in the kind of miniature allegory he would come to call 'double-level' writing (*VP* 8).[24]

Analogous concerns are apparent in MacNeice's BBC features. His radio drama has largely been neglected by readers of his poetry, yet it constitutes a significant body of writing: he wrote 'more than 120 scripts' during the twenty-two years he worked for the BBC, the majority of which remain unpublished (*Plays*, xi).[25] As Heuser and McDonald argue, these plays demand to be read alongside the poems, and share 'complex resonances and ambiguities' with them (*Plays*, xiv). To give a snapshot of these interconnections, I consider one of MacNeice's most successful and characteristic wartime features.

He Had a Date responds to the death of MacNeice's school friend, Graham Shepard, who was lost at sea when his corvette the HMS *Polyanthus* was torpedoed in the Atlantic in September 1943.[26] Shepard was the subject of one of *Springboard*'s longer poems, 'The Casualty'. The protagonist of *He Had a Date* is someone 'typical of his period', whom listeners might even dismiss 'as a fool, a failure, or even a cad' (*Plays*, 75). As an 'uneasy intellectual from the upper classes', Tom Varney's story mirrors the major events of his period (*Plays*, 71). The play is punctuated by references to suffragettes, the General Strike, the Spanish Civil War (in which Tom fights against the fascists) and both world wars. To use one of the play's organizing naval metaphors, these are the external 'bearings' through which Tom's journey is plotted. He is pulled by antithetical impulses. While at Oxford, he oscillates between academic ambition and reaction against his class after meeting a striker who points out his ignorance of the realities of working-class life. After marrying a working-class girl, Tom finds himself unable to communicate with her. Like the characters of *Springboard*, Tom's dilemma is of commitment. On the outbreak of the Second World War, he reflects that Spain 'was my war. But this? Is this my war or not?' (*Plays*, 100). MacNeice had asked himself the same question in letters to E. R. Dodds in October 1939: 'I am beginning to think this may be *my* war after all ... *if* it is my war, I feel I ought to get involved in it in one of the more unpleasant ways'.[27] Though MacNeice could not do this himself, texts like *He Had a Date* and 'The Casualty' pay undeceived tribute to those who did; indeed, the play is all the more impressive for its refusal to *varnish* Tom Varney into something he was not. As in 'The Casualty' and 'The Springboard', MacNeice's *exempla* of moral courage are unconvinced and unconvincing figures who are the more credible because of their weaknesses.[28]

SWANSEA UNIVERSITY LIBRARY

WITHDRAWN

He Had a Date also illustrates the influence of radio work on MacNeice's poetry. The play is structured through the use of flashback: as Tom drowns, he revisits his life as a sequence of overlapping conversations. In the introduction to *Sunbeams in his Hat* (a feature on Chekhov originally written in 1941 as a compliment to the USSR on joining the war) MacNeice considered the pros and cons of the device:

> For this programme I used the method of the *flash-back*. [...] This method can be confusing and irritating, though when it comes off it provides tension and unity [...] larger-than-lifeness need not be part of the recipe; in a programme called *He Had a Date* I attempted the chronicle of a fictitious young man of our time and characterised him throughout by understatement and, while I did not succeed with him, I see nothing wrong in the method (*DT* 69–70)

MacNeice connects flashback with his desire to avoid 'larger-than-lifeness': the 'tension and unity' of the flashback enables the writer to construct a convincing aural portrait. As Heuser and McDonald point out, 'Radio drama was not simply to be poetry by other means'; crucially, the artifice of flashback enabled MacNeice to characterize Tom 'by understatement' (*Plays*, xii). As I have already suggested, understatement became increasingly prominent in MacNeice's poetry. 'The Casualty' (*CP* 237–40) shows him adapting tools he had used in the writing and production of radio features for the construction of an elegy. In place of flashback, the poem uses 'snapshots' from Shepard's life:

> Here you are swapping gags in winking bars
> With half an eye on the colour clash of beet
> Lobster and radish, here you are talking back
> To a caged baboon and here the Wiltshire sleet
> Riddles your football jersey – here the sack
> Of night pours down on you Provençal stars.
>
> Here you are gabbling Baudelaire or Donne,
> Here you are mimicking that cuckoo clock,
> Here you are serving a double fault for set,
> Here you are diving naked from a Dalmatian rock,
> Here you are barracking the sinking sun,
> Here you are taking Proust aboard your doomed corvette.

By juxtaposing different moments from Shepard's life, Mac-Neice gives a dynamic sense of an individual. Like Tom Varney and other characters in *Springboard*, Graham Shepard emerges as an unremarkable man of his time, whose life was taken out of his own control by the war. There is no sense that 'taking Proust aboard your doomed corvette' is heroic. Rather, the end of Shepard's life is of a piece with events like 'swapping gags in winking bars' or 'serving a double fault for set'. Critics have faulted 'The Casualty' for its absence of heroic rhetoric, yet the truth is that the poem, like the radio features MacNeice was working on during the 1940s, deliberately avoids any such inflation.[29] In MacNeice's perhaps overly puritanical view, to inflate was to falsify. These prosaic yet elegantly phrased snapshots serve both to capture his memories of Shepard and more broadly to elegize the losses of the war.

LONGING FOR WHAT WAS NEVER HOME: THE POETRY OF NOSTALGIA

Readers of *Springboard* might have expected the end of the war to stimulate MacNeice to reflect the optimistic mood of the time, especially with the election of Clement Attlee's radical Labour government in July 1945. Yet *Holes in the Sky* views the post-war world with a mixture of contempt and disillusion. 'The Streets of Laredo' scarcely recognizes the end of the war, as a 'pancaked' London is a theatre for profiteering and parochialism; 'Aftermath' laments the loss of a communal fear of death which led to social solidarity between 'the child/ Of luck' and 'the child of lack'; 'Bluebells' contrasts the anticipation of a couple separated by the war with the bleaker reality of their reunion (CP 253–5). 'Hiatus' (written, like 'The Streets of Laredo', in July 1945) sees the war as 'The years that did not count' which have interrupted the maturation of a generation:

> The schoolboys of the Thirties reappear,
> Fledged in the void, indubitably men,
> Having kept vigil on the Unholy Mount
> And found some dark and tentative things made clear,
> Some clear made dark, in the years that did not count.

(CP 254)

103

To be 'Fledged in the void' is to be cut adrift both from the past and from the comfort zone of youth. As 'indubitably men', MacNeice and his contemporaries can no longer bank on unfulfilled potential. 'Hiatus' raises a concern which runs through *Plant and Phantom*, *Springboard* and *Holes in the Sky*: a critical nostalgia for childhood and a hankering to make poetic sense of these undigested experiences. Though apparently distinct from the concerns of allegiance and wartime, it is a mistake to decouple these subjective poems from the contexts in which they were written. *The Strings are False* clarifies the connection: from the early 1940s, MacNeice looks back to his childhood on the supposition that 'everyone' is 'in a muddle' and that 'I shall find my life is not just mine, that it mirrors the lives of others' (*SF* 35). The feeling of having grown up, of no longer being a promising schoolboy, is inextricably connected with the ambiguities of 'The years which did not count'.

MacNeice's revisiting of childhood entails overlapping memories of two world wars; as 'Carrick Revisited' asks: 'Which war was which?' Such bewilderment intimates a central preoccupation of these poems: that the remembered past is delusive, that nostalgia dangerously replaces the actual with the idealized. 'Nostalgia' itself suggests that 'the times at which/ The will is vulnerable' leave us open to a 'longing/ For what was never home' (*CP* 227). Home is an unstable property in MacNeice's poems of childhood, which tend to be bleak and unsentimental, in the same key as *The Strings are False*, overshadowed by the guilts and terrors of childhood. 'Autobiography' (*CP* 201) renders childhood trauma through the sing-song lilt of nursery rhyme rhythms and the enigmatic jingle of its refrain:

> When my silent terror cried,
> Nobody, nobody replied.
>
> *Come back early or never come.*

The past is occluded in the deliberate repression of the word 'home'; through a line framed by the rhyming 'come', MacNeice gestures towards the speaker's inability to 'come home'.[30] Like 'Autobiography', 'Christina' (also from *Plant and Phantom*; *CP* 190–1) is light verse at its most grimly serious. Fusing memories of the nursery with adult sexuality alongside the familiar

104

rhythms and syntax of nursery rhyme, the poem makes a liaison between childhood play and sexual dysfunction:

> He went to bed with a lady
> Somewhere seen before,
> He heard the name Christina
> And suddenly saw Christina
> Dead on the nursery floor.

MacNeice's point is again that the nursery is not a secure haven. What the child does to the doll – 'She smiled when you dressed her/ And when you then undressed her/ She kept a smiling face' – the man does to the woman; the poem is animated by the uncomfortable sense that the 'lady' is as much of a 'dead' object as the broken doll. Similarly, *The Strings are False* records the young MacNeice committing 'a murder' by accidentally capsizing a bird's nest: 'I cannot remember seeing the nestlings fall out, but when I came past there again, there they were hanging in the hedge, little naked corpses, terrible, silent' (*SF* 55). Such texts reveal the individual as shaped by feelings of unappeasable guilt within an environment which cannot hide the violence of the world beyond the gates of the rectory.

So for MacNeice, childhood was not separable from the full range of adult experience. *Springboard* embodies this perception in the structure of the volume, which is bookended by 'Prayer Before Birth' and 'Postscript' (later titled 'When We Were Children'). Though these poems may look out of place in the wartime context of the rest of the volume, by bracketing the war poems with these texts, MacNeice stresses the interplay between the past and the present both for himself as an individual and for society as a whole. 'Prayer Before Birth' (*CP* 213–14) looks outward from the individual to the community s/he will join; from the perspective of an unborn child, the poem castigates a world deformed by authoritarianism and mechanization:

> I am not yet born; O hear me,
> Let not the man who is beast or who thinks he is God
>   come near me.
>
> I am not yet born; O fill me
> With strength against those who would freeze my
>   humanity, would dragoon me into a lethal automaton,
>   would make me a cog in a machine, a thing with
>   one face

'Prayer Before Birth' is a disillusioned account of socialization, in which the individual is systematically victimized by a series of impersonal aggressors. It becomes a critical lament, which guardedly maintains through its rhetorical structure as a prayer some limited hope for the future. We may avoid the man 'who thinks he is God'; we do not have to become 'lethal automatons'. Yet in the mechanistic, pyramidal structure of each stanza, where new clauses are ratcheted into place with a crazy efficiency, and the individual is blown 'like thistledown hither and/ thither or hither and thither', the poem ominously reflects the larger forces which delimit human autonomy.

In contrast, 'Postscript' (*CP* 250) initially evokes a simpler time. The poem captures the excitement of language acquisition, when words were charged with sensuous value: 'Harlot and murder were dark purple'. It reimagines the thrill of discovering a landscape: 'When we were children Spring was easy,/ Dousing our heads in suds of hawthorn/ And scrambling the laburnum tree'. Yet this nostalgic excursion is contained by the intrusion of the present, 'Whose winds and sweets have now forsaken/ Lungs that are black, tongues that are dry'. While at one level this is a simple recognition of the passage of time, in the context of the volume, it is hard to read 'Lungs that are black, tongues that are dry' without being reminded of warfare. 'Postscript' is both the final word of *Springboard* and a tailpiece to the second part of the collection, including 'The Casualty' and the long sectional poem 'The Kingdom', which praises a putative 'Kingdom of individuals', who resist 'the crust of bureaucracy' (*CP* 241). 'Postscript' is poised between the optimism of 'The Kingdom' and the elegiac mood of 'The Casualty'. By the final stanza, 'Now we are older [...]/ To handsel joy requires a new/ Shuffle of cards behind the brain'; MacNeice does not rule out the possibility of joy, but the process whereby 'meaning shall remarry colour/ And flowers be timeless once again' is not specified. Like the 'thirst' potentially accentuated by the liberal poets, 'Postscript' conceives of a positive future through sleight of hand rather than through the hollow rhetoric of heroism or poetic braggadocio. This 'new/ Shuffle' might be the sceptic's best response to the cynic's 'So what?'

5

Waiting for the Thaw: The Later MacNeice

During the 'Dialogue with my Guardian Angel' from *I Crossed the Minch*, the Angel accuses MacNeice of abstraction from the real world. Instead of assenting to the Angel's social realism – 'Reading's a place where they make biscuits' – MacNeice favours an 'astigmatic and purblind intellectual concept of what a biscuit factory is, might have been, ought to be or can't be' (*ICM* 135).[1] As the exchange becomes more abusive, the Angel insists:

> G.A. [...] You know what you're like? You're like a snowman waiting for the thaw.
> ME: There's nothing else a snowman can do.

For the Angel, the snowman embodies MacNeice's dilettantism, his culpable preference for disengagement over commitment. For MacNeice, the Angel misconstrues his own metaphor, as he wants the snowman to represent an obduracy alien to its substance. When the Angel suggests that MacNeice would 'go on standing out there as a snowman [...] getting colder and colder', he tartly rejoins 'If it's getting colder and colder, there won't be any thaw' (*ICM* 135–6). The snowman is contestable property, evoking ideas both of deep-frozen stasis and over-night change. Though the issues underlying the 'Dialogue' – whether the writer should embrace communism – receded after the 1930s, the analogy resurfaced over twenty years later in 'The Snow Man' (*CP* 564–5), from *Solstices*.[2] Appropriately enough, the image becomes a way of understanding the individual's relationship with his past: 'His memory was shaped by forgetting/ Into a snowman'. As before, the image is tendentious and provokes interrogation:

> But was this fellow really his past,
> This white dummy in a white waste?
> While the censor works, while the frost holds,
> Perhaps he will pass – but then he will pass.

Snowmen are part of the comforting, chintzy paraphernalia of childhood Christmases, yet in MacNeice's hands, the image gains a disturbing timbre.[3] If memory can be represented by a snowman, it becomes 'a white waste': the line suggests the occlusion of the past as well as its fundamental inarticulacy. The snowman is a 'white dummy', however comic he might look. Though the analogy 'will pass', in that it will make sense, the snowman itself 'will pass' because he must thaw. This paratactic deployment of different meanings of the same word is characteristic of MacNeice's later work. Through its verbal self-consciousness, the poem emphasizes semantic slippage to make the reader conscious of the different resonances within the same word:

> Today is a legless day with head-on
> Idiot eyes, a stranded deaf
> Mute in a muted world. This lump
> Is what he remembered when he forgot,
>
> Already beginning to dribble. Tomorrow
> Comes the complete forgetting, the thaw.
> Or is it rather a dance of water
> To replace, relive, that dance of white?

As the poem unfolds, MacNeice finds in the analogy a grotesque similarity between the snowman and the ageing process. Semantic juxtaposition heightens the process of defamiliarization: all snowmen are 'legless', yet 'Today is a legless day' conveys the sense of a man suffering from a hangover 'stranded [...] in a muted world'. Similarly, the next sentence conflates the thawing of the snowman with the gradual erosion of the man's memory, as the 'lump' of forgotten memories begins 'to dribble'. In this case, the description of thawing carries darker intimations of senility, a loss of physical as well as mental control. Even so, despite the shortfall between the remembered snowman and the actuality of ageing, the poem ends ambiguously. The final question holds open whether the thaw will lead to 'the complete forgetting', which would presumably entail the loss of identity, or the 'reliving' of 'that dance of white'.

'The Snow Man' voices issues which preoccupied MacNeice throughout the 1950s and early 1960s. It is concerned with the sense we make of the past and the relationship between innocence and experience. Like so many of his later poems, it views this relationship darkly, from the perspective of a soured and disappointed maturity. In its reworking of *I Crossed the Minch*, the poem exemplifies the revisiting of earlier artistic motifs. MacNeice never left his past alone; he recycled similar incidents and images throughout his career. Yet this process coexists with an impulse to experiment. As his understanding of the past was dynamic, so he looked for different poetic forms to convey his changing perspectives. Thus 'The Snow Man' is a parable, the form of miniature allegory or 'double-level writing' which would become so prominent in his later volumes.

LOST GENERATIONS?

By the end of the war, MacNeice was acutely conscious of the ways in which the passage of time must change 'The schoolboys of the Thirties'. Critics have generally found the poetry of the late 1940s and early 1950s the least satisfactory part of his output. 'Day of Renewal' admits 'This middle stretch/ Of life is bad for poets' (CP 349); most readers have needed little prompting to agree. Defending his decision to include nothing from *Ten Burnt Offerings* and *Autumn Sequel* in his selected MacNeice, Auden suggested, 'in the early nineteen-fifties, Louis MacNeice struck a bad patch [...] I would not call the poems from this period bad [...] but I do find them a bit dull'.[4] For Edna Longley, MacNeice suffered 'from an attack of wordiness in the late 1940s and early 1950s'.[5] There have been exceptions to this consensus: John Montague surprised MacNeice by telling him that Thomas Kinsella preferred *Autumn Sequel* to *Autumn Journal*; McDonald has argued that both *Ten Burnt Offerings* and *Autumn Sequel* are a necessary experimental prelude to the success of MacNeice's final three volumes.[6] This revisionism informs my approach to this work. Although these longer poems of the 'middle stretch' are unlikely to challenge the popularity of short poems like 'Snow' or 'Bagpipe Music', they remain, as Auden conceded, 'beautifully carpentered' and artistically adventurous in ways which shape subsequent poems. In both their experimental forms and their self-conscious content, these texts show MacNeice in the act of responding to the passage of time and changes in literary fashion.

His later criticism betrays a ruminative anxiety about the placement of his generation in literary history. In a review of G. S. Fraser's *Poetry Now* anthology, provocatively titled 'Lost Generations?' (1957), MacNeice protests against the 'game of pigeonholing literary generations' (*SLC* 206–11).[7] While he thanks Fraser 'for not treating the "Thirties" as a dirty or non-U phrase' ('non-U' is a piece of 1950s argot meaning socially or culturally unacceptable),[8] MacNeice rubbishes his literary history, which defines Auden and MacNeice as 'Augustans' who were superseded by 'Romantics': 'Posterity may find our generations closer to each other than we care to think'. In considering Fraser's advocacy of Movement poets who came to prominence during the 1950s, MacNeice is sceptical about group aesthetics:

> these better ones [Elizabeth Jennings, John Holloway and Philip Larkin] strike me as *individual* poets; it is not their group characteristics which make them interesting. The chief characteristics of the 'Movement', we are often told, are neatness and lucidity. But are these so new in our time? To mention just one name from many, what about the late Norman Cameron? Surely any professional poet, grouped or ungrouped, dated or dateless, ought to be able, *when he chooses*, to be neat or lucid, or both

Though MacNeice displays the professional irritation of the poet at the anthologist (whose work necessarily simplifies individual poets), as an act of 'sticking-out-of-the-neck', the review articulates key preconceptions and anxieties. The emphasis on the individual poet underlines MacNeice's sense that the poets of the 1930s were a diverse generation rather than a group who shared an homogenous aesthetic. By suggesting that the same applies to the poets of the Movement, he queries the credibility of such shorthands.

MacNeice identifies a problem at the heart of contemporary criticism: how should criticism mediate the enormous range of poems to a broad reading public?[9] Literary generations are convenient categorizing devices which enable critics to generalize without the need to provide nuanced accounts of each writer. By singling out Norman Cameron, MacNeice draws attention to the pitfalls of presenting poets in this way. Cameron was a fringe player in the literary coteries of the time, who enjoyed friendships with a broad range of writers including Dylan Thomas and MacNeice.[10] From a Scottish colonial background, Cameron was another poet of the educated upper-middle classes. While at Oxford, he published alongside MacNeice, Auden, Spender and Day Lewis in *Oxford Poetry*. During the 1930s, his work appeared in *New Verse* and was read enthusiastically by other writers; in *Modern Poetry*, MacNeice praised him alongside his friends Laura Riding and Robert Graves as one of the 'few poets to-day who [...] philosophize in their poetry' (*MP* 112–13). Despite sharing networks with Auden and MacNeice (he coined the infamous joke that Spender was 'the Rupert Brooke of the Depression'), Cameron's work remains largely uninfluenced by them. As a result, he tends to be overlooked in surveys of the period, as MacNeice's review anticipated.[11] In Jonathan Barker's useful formulation, Cameron's poems 'are concise moral tales able to buttonhole the reader in the manner of biblical parables'. 'Public-House Confidence', 'The Compassionate Fool' and 'Naked Among the Trees' (all published during the 1930s) exemplify a poetry of 'neatness and lucidity', and partly anticipate Larkin's work, as well as that of the later MacNeice.[12]

But this allusion also intimates a sense of generational loss which becomes explicit in *Autumn Sequel*. Cameron died in 1953, and MacNeice registers that he is already a voice of the past. In addition to its elegy for Dylan Thomas (one of the few passages in the poem to have enjoyed widespread praise), *Autumn Sequel* offers a tribute to Cameron as MacNeice revisits Oxford:

> taking one last stroll along the Turl,
> Half savouring the mist and my own gloom
>
> I pass the shop where Esther, a slim girl,
> Chose herself roses for a ball and pass
> The rooms where one young poet used to twirl
>
> His inconclusions in a whisky glass,
> A tall and tousled man who wrote short poems and died
> This summer. Oxford trees weep leaves on Oxford grass
>
> Suggesting a tag of Homer.

(*CP* 431–2)

'Esther' is readily identified as MacNeice's first wife, Mary.[13] Though the poet is unnamed, this appropriately terse elegy leaves little doubt that MacNeice had Cameron in mind. As the brevity of his verse was a defining literary characteristic, so his stature was a distinguishing physical feature: 'Norman was a huge chap', as one friend put it.[14] The connection of Mary with Cameron suggests the nexus of issues at stake for MacNeice in remembering the Oxford of the late 1920s. Mary was 'the best dancer in Oxford'; 'Sunlight in the Garden' had used dance to articulate the end of their relationship: 'And soon, my friend,/ We shall have no time for dances' (SF 31; CP 57). In this case, by juxtaposing Mary choosing 'roses for a ball' with Cameron 'twirl[ing]/ His inconclusions in a whisky glass', MacNeice combines the fate of his marriage with the fate of one member of his literary generation.

This return to Oxford is explicitly elegiac: the previous canto evokes the disappearance of 'the clique/ That you yourself in Nineteen-twenty-six [...] belonged to', and links the death of Shepard with the emigration of Auden: 'Now Egdon lives across that same Atlantic/ Where Gavin met his death' (CP 427–8). Although there is little reproach in this coupling, it is significant that Auden/ Egdon's emigration makes him as inaccessible as Shepard/ Gavin's drowning. The pervasive presence of the elegiac mode in the poem, alongside what McDonald calls 'celebration', means that *Autumn Sequel* is best understood in the terms of its subtitle as 'A Rhetorical Poem'.[15] It is permeated by rhetorical gestures and shaped by its status as a sequel to *Autumn Journal*. The Oxford passage is an exercise in the classical trope of *ubi sunt* ('where are they now?') in the voice of the Parrot, a symbol of truistic pseudo-wisdom, which nihilistically enumerates transience and flux: 'Everything flows. And dries. So runs that old Greek moral/ Which Parrot loves to bandy week by week' (CP 427). In *The Burning Perch*, Parrot mutates into 'Budgie', one of MacNeice's final satires of a culture dominated by narcissism, television and the detritus of other peoples' ideas and formulations: 'all the world is a stage is a cage/ A hermitage a fashion show a crèche an auditorium/ Or possibly a space ship' (CP 602). In both poems, the voice of the caged bird relentlessly recycles, or twitters, the second-hand, the truistic and the false.

The rhetoric of *Autumn Sequel* is connected with revisiting: from the outset, MacNeice critiques *Autumn Journal*. The first canto deplores 'each megrim and moan I scrawled on the sky/ In my hand of unformed smoke those fifteen years/ A-going, a-going, ago', and distances the reader from the postures MacNeice and his contemporaries adopted: 'Did we know/ That when that came which we had said would come,/ We still should be proved wrong?' (CP 373, 376). This is the most rhetorical of rhetorical questions: the text leaves the reader no room to disagree; we must collaborate with the apparently superior wisdom of 1953 over 1938.

Autumn Sequel sharply poses the question of the viability of sequels. For Longley, it 'proves that, artistically speaking, you can never go back'.[16] Yet, as McDonald suggests, the poem's rhetoricity, along with its use of the intricate form of *terza rima* 'seems almost calculated to offend the critical orthodoxies of the mid-1950s'.[17] More pressingly, the poem is almost calculated to offend those readers who had enjoyed *Autumn Journal*. Writing the earlier poem off as 'each megrim and moan' is at once gruffly eloquent and more dismissive than that poem's harshest critics. By shortcircuiting *Autumn Journal*, *Autumn Sequel* para-doxically banks on readers' knowledge of the earlier text, and a readiness to have it superseded. Yet *Autumn Sequel* is tonally distinct from its predecessor. It does not develop out of light verse; rather, the 'rhetorical' aspect of the later poem responds to and rebukes the 'journal' form of its predecessor.

The problem remains how to react to such self-conscious wordiness. To an extent, this depends on poetic context: the reader must distinguish between the mechanistic utterances of the Parrot and the voice of the poet which attempts 'To contrive the truth' via the tricks and resources of language (CP 374). As McDonald rightly observes, *Autumn Sequel* becomes 'a paradox-ical undertaking', in which the reader must be acutely sensitive to tone, speaking voice and poetic idiom.[18] The poem stands or falls on the strength of its rhetoric, the extent to which readers can endorse or critically evaluate its linguistic contrivances. It attempts to achieve a density of expression which is capable of admonishing the vulgarities of the modern world while at the same time paying tribute to 'Everydayness' and resisting nihilistic impulses (CP 397). This is, to put it mildly, a difficult task, especially since the historical context of the autumn of 1953 was so much less personally involving than that of 1938. Though registering events such as the Korean War and the beginning of 'experimental bombing' in Kenya, these events are experienced at second hand and do not impinge on the relatively privileged life of the poet-speaker (*CP* 460). Where the humanism of *Autumn Journal* is ballasted by a sense of national panic and by the improvisational cast of its ethical formulations, *Autumn Sequel* generates its impetus more from the poet's personal preoccupations – his friends, his job, and his own values.

This is not necessarily a handicap, but it does mean that the poem's 'celebrations' must generate their own sense of significance. The virtues and vices of *Autumn Sequel* can be shown by a passage like the end of Canto VII, the 'Fanfare for the Makers'. These makers are more than just poets: they are individuals who 'turned their cosmic guilt to cosmic pride' by resisting the blandishments of the 'Antagonist' and the Parrot:

> So Fanfare for the Makers: who compose
> A book of words or deeds who runs may write
> As many do who run, as a family grows
>
> At times like sunflowers turning towards the light,
> As sometimes in the blackout and the raids
> One joke composed an island in the night
>
> [...]
>
> As mothers sit up late night after night
> Moulding a life, as miners day by day
> Descend blind shafts, as a boy may flaunt his kite
>
> In an empty nonchalant sky, as anglers play
> Their fish, as workers work and can take pride
> In spending sweat before they draw their pay,
>
> As horsemen fashion horses while they ride,
> As climbers climb a peak because it is there,
> As life can be confirmed even in suicide:
>
> To make is such. Let us make. And set the weather fair.
>
> (*CP* 405–6)

In many ways, the thinking of *Autumn Sequel* is directly congruent with that of *Autumn Journal*. Where the earlier poem rebukes 'the wish to quit', the later poem affirms the value of life as a constructive activity, in which literary composition metaphorically evokes a range of activities, from bearing children to mining to even angling (*CP* 154). Equally, the jokes 'in the blackout and the raids' suggest some continuity in terms of the poetic handling of major historical events. Yet the expression of *Autumn Sequel* is rooted in a different key from its predecessor. *Autumn Journal* acknowledges when its 'phrases' become 'high falutin' and recurs to conversational rhythms and expression; in *Autumn Sequel*, the 'high falutin' is largely unqualified. This can pay generous poetic dividends: the graceful syntactic self-involvement of this passage shows MacNeice expertly managing the interlacing rhymes of *terza rima* before producing a climactic line of three short sentences. As in the Cameron elegy, the paradox of *Autumn Sequel* is that its leisurely syntax can achieve moments of pithy, epigrammatic condensation. Yet the poem's verbal texture remains more conventionally poetic than any of MacNeice's other major works. Phrases like 'as a boy may flaunt his kite/ In an empty nonchalant sky' and 'As horsemen fashion horses while they ride' have a traditional poetic flash which recalls poets as diverse as Marlowe and Yeats. The traditional cast of the text was underlined when Helen Gardner (a former colleague of MacNeice's at Birmingham) used it as an Epilogue to her *New Oxford Book of English Verse*. Read in that context – a context which includes William Dunbar's 'Lament for the Makeris', the poem from which MacNeice's takes its prompt – the activity of making is redirected towards the art of poetry. 'A Fanfare for the Makers', as Gardner titled it, becomes a defence of poetry through life, rather than, as MacNeice had framed it, a defence of life through poetry.[19] Nevertheless, the paradoxical and self-contradictory quality of MacNeice's thinking remain prominent. The key line, 'As life can be confirmed even in suicide', anticipates the much riskier and experimental exploration of suicide as a creative act in 'The Suicide'.

FROM *TEN BURNT OFFERINGS* TO THE LATER POEMS

Autumn Sequel was reviewed as evidence of the last gasp of an exhausted generation. A. Alvarez connected the diffuseness of

Autumn Sequel with Auden's *The Age of Anxiety*, arguing that 'All we can do is, with them, lament the makers they might have been'.[20] Yet, as the Fanfare indicates, lament coexists with celebration. Moreover, although the rhyming structure of *Autumn Sequel* fosters the deployment of a more traditional poetic rhetoric, it shows MacNeice's ongoing absorption with questions of technique and his refusal to settle for predictable effects.

Experimentalism is also prominent in *Ten Burnt Offerings*. Like the longer poems of the later 1940s, these texts show an interest in the work of Eliot and Rilke. In an essay of 1949, MacNeice connects 'The Stygian Banks', from *Holes in the Sky*, with Rilke's *Duino Elegies*, admitting that 'Such poems are tentative [...] essays in the genre in which Rilke achieved such astonishing exactitude' (*SLC* 163).[21] *Ten Burnt Offerings* develops this interest through a sequence of ten poems, each with four sections, each of which deploys different forms and intertwines contrasting voices and perspectives. At their best, these poems can be ambitious and suggestive, as in 'Didymus', which shows MacNeice creatively amalgamating his experience of India (which he visited to report on the end of colonial rule) with a mythopoeic interest in the legend that Doubting Thomas established the Christian church in Kerala. Equally, 'Didymus' exemplifies the lapse of experimentation into formalism:

> Whatever the clime, my task is ever to climb
>> Foothills that never are mountains; this Indian sky
> Is bowed with the dour monsoon and I doubt but soon
>> All of my converts and most of my work must die.
>
> (*CP* 335)

Each stanza of this section deploys elaborate *rime riche*: 'clime' gives way to 'climb', as elsewhere 'role' to 'roll' and 'sore' to 'soar'. Though 'beautifully carpentered', here carpentry dictates effect: the overall impression is one of a poetic exhibition rather than of a text in which there is a dynamic give and take between form and meaning.

Nevertheless, *Ten Burnt Offerings* feeds directly into more successful texts in *Visitations*, *Solstices* and *The Burning Perch*. Sectional poems like 'Jigsaws', 'Notes for a Biography', 'Indoor Sports', 'Nature Notes', 'As In Their Time' and 'Memorandum to

Horace' manage their formal impulses with greater elasticity and a sharper sense of poetic freedom, while the linguistic and formal self-consciousness of *Ten Burnt Offerings* informs a range of shorter poems in the final volumes. 'Wordiness' is still present in the later poems, though deployed to greater purpose. Consider the use of nursery rhyme in 'Day of Renewal' (*CP* 350–2), a poem which Longley accuses of managing to make MacNeice's 'autobiography uninteresting'.[22] The second section uses the Dick Whittington story to recollect infancy through a schizophrenic fantasia of nursery texts:

> We are still children;
> Don't Care was hung, Did Care was haunted;
> Big A, Little A, Why's in the cupboard;
> Why, say the children, is Why in the cupboard?

> (*CP* 351–2)

Such writing shows MacNeice in the process of realizing the potential force of nursery rhymes without fully communicating anything new to his readers. As I noted in chapter 1, 'Notes for a Biography' uses a more restricted palette of nursery rhymes as structuring metaphors for the life of a colonial administrator. More radically, 'Château Jackson' rewrites 'The House that Jack Built' (*CP* 580–1) as an ambiguous modern 'quest'. The poem is formally extreme in using only monosyllables and a relentless rhythm which is at once perfectly controlled and maddeningly monotonous:

> Where is the Jack that built the house
> That housed the folk that tilled the field
> That filled the bags that brimmed the mill
> That ground the flour that browned the bread
> That fed the serfs that scrubbed the floors
> That wore the mats that kissed the feet
> That bore the bums that raised the heads [...]

The chief difference between this poem and 'Day of Renewal' is in terms of the urgency gained from focusing on a single nursery rhyme. Banking on the familiarity of the original text, MacNeice unsettles the reader at every turn: Jack becomes 'the Jack', suggesting that he is an amorphous property rather than a recognizable individual, and perhaps recalling the Elizabethan slang, in which a 'jack' is a social climber.[23] This agenda is clear

117

in succeeding lines, as Jack's house is placed in a broader economic structure in which bags are filled, serfs are fed and feet are kissed. Instead of the familiar pastoral enumerations of the original rhyme, MacNeice offers a dysfunctional parable which finally shades into epitaph: 'That bears the slab that wears the words/ That tell the truth that ends the quest'. Even *rime riche* is more successfully deployed here, as 'tilled the *field*' fades into '*filled* the bags'.[24] 'Château Jackson' explicitly glances back to *Ten Burnt Offerings*: 'That drees the weird that scoops the news' quotes from that volume's short prefatory text: 'Every poem drees its weird' (*CP* 314). To dree one's weird is to undergo one's fate: this pointed self-quotation suggests that this ambiguous process remained at the core of what MacNeice believed he was doing as a writer during the 1950s and 1960s.[25]

If the linguistic self-consciousness of *Ten Burnt Offerings* inflects later poems, so does its propensity for elaborate structures. 'Dark Age Glosses', 'Indoor Sports' and 'Nature Notes', from *Solstices*, are shorter sequences, but they are equally absorbed by the quest to explore new formal patterns. 'Nature Notes' (*CP* 548–9) is particularly significant in the context of the failed autobiography of 'Day of Renewal' in that it shows MacNeice discovering an original way of revisiting his past. The poem takes the form of four different 'notes', all of which conform to the same pattern. Dandelions, Cats, Corncrakes and The Sea are described in the same or cognate terms; their description overlaps with the evocation of MacNeice's childhood:

> *Corncrakes*
>
> Incorrigible, unmusical,
> They bridged the surrounding hedge of my childhood,
> Unsubtle, the opposite of blackbirds,
> But, unlike blackbirds, capable
> Anywhere they are of endorsing summer
> Like loud men around the corner
> Whom we never see but whose raucous
> Voices can give us confidence.

> *The Sea*
>
> Incorrigible, ruthless,
> It rattled the shingly beach of my childhood,
> Subtle, the opposite of earth,

> And, unlike earth, capable
> Any time at all of proclaiming eternity
> Like something or someone to whom
> We have to surrender, finding
> Through that surrender life.

The pattern of 'Nature Notes' is at once constricting and conversational. As in his strongest writing, MacNeice makes a compromise between a credible speaking voice and a poetic register distinct from the ordinary or truistic. Unlike the poems of *Ten Burnt Offerings*, however, 'Nature Notes' does not attempt to be anything more than a sequence of loosely linked jottings. It makes no pretensions to a comprehensive evocation of the Northern Irish topography of MacNeice's childhood nor to the things it describes.[26] Yet in its light touch and the formal liaisons it establishes between each note, the poem lets the reader consider similarities and differences between ostensibly un-related objects. All of them are 'Incorrigible', they are alternately 'Unsubtle' or 'Subtle'; MacNeice's repeated adjectives and recurring syntax imply the contrasting values of the different objects and the almost cultic value which they have for his speaker. For each note, the thing described is both a subject of nostalgia and, through the formula of each closing simile, a suggestion of realities beyond the 'hedge of my childhood'.

This suggests the ways in which MacNeice realized that sectional poems could be vehicles for the exploration of questions of identity and commitment. Though 'Nature Notes' is far removed from political discourse, its similes make connections between the natural world and wider emotional commitments. Cats are an education in erotic good manners: 'Like women who want no contract/ But going their own way/ Make the way of their lovers lighter'. Similarly, the closing image of 'finding/ Through that surrender life' conveys a broader sense of ethical priority similar to the existential humanism of 'Thalassa'. In other poems, the contemporary political context comes through more convincingly than it had in either *Ten Burnt Offerings* or *Autumn Sequel*. 'Notes for a Biography' articulates a first reaction to the dropping of the atom bomb on Hiroshima and Nagasaki:

> '[...] look, here is Japan
> Where man must now make what he chooses of man,

And these towns are selected to pay for their crime –
A milestone in history, a gravestone in time.'

When I first read the news, to my shame I was glad;
When I next read the news I thought man had gone mad,
And every day since the more news that I read
I too would plead guilty – but where can I plead?

(*CP* 531)

The elastic form of the sectional poem enables MacNeice to capture the horror of nuclear war through a return to the anapaestic lilt and full rhymes of light verse. Inevitably, the return to a lighter idiom is bitterly sardonic: the poem critically juxtaposes a jocose poetic idiom with terrible events. If 'Nature Notes' shows MacNeice using sectional form to return to aspects of his past, 'Notes for Biography' shows how similar forms could be used to explore the crisis of values provoked by nuclear warfare.

'Notes for a Biography' raises questions about the kind of poetry MacNeice produced in the last three volumes. The poem hovers between a schematic depiction of its subject as a cipher for his class – 'Schooled to service (or was it a pride of class?)/ He graduated at length to a land of babus and banyans' – and a more sympathetic portrayal of him as a moral agent in the section on the bombing of Japan. Yet that concludes feebly with the admission that the speaker is 'Outnumbered, outmoded', and the bathetic prayer that 'Common sense, if not love, will still carry the day' (*CP* 529, 531). Though MacNeice is widely viewed as a poet of common sense, the poems of *The Burning Perch* in particular open up more radical queries of common-sensical thinking and the idea of a unitary or coherent self.[27] 'As In Their Time' (*CP* 598–601) is a fine example of this scepticism. It is an extreme combination of sectional form with linguistic self-consciousness. Divided into twelve, independent, five-line miniatures, cumulatively the poem conveys a chaotic sense of the 'time' in which its protagonists live: it is another generational poem, keyed to the anxieties of a particular time. Like 'Nature Notes', these conversational shorts are elaborately structured as MacNeice interrogates assumptions underlying conventional idioms:

> She believed in love, but was it
> Her self or her role believed?
> And was it believed and not
> Professed or envied? Lastly,
> Was it love she believed in?

An ostensibly simple proposition is dissected, queried and ultimately discarded. 'She believed in love', but the questions which follow undermine any certainty of the phrase's meaning. There is no convincing distinction between 'Her self' and 'her role', while the verb of active commitment – 'believed in' – is equally hollow, weakly masquerading for darker alternatives like 'Professed or envied'. As a sequence, 'As In Their Time' is an exercise in the stripping away of excuses by exposing the poverty of their semantics. One section sardonically condenses the mental processes of left-leaning intellectuals like MacNeice himself:

> For what it was worth he had to
> Make a recurring protest:
> Which was at least a gesture
> Which was a vindication
> Or excuse for what it was worth.

Recalling earlier poems like 'Bottleneck', this text explores the processes of self-deception by rehearsing the characteristic gestures of a stratum of post-war British society. The protagonist wearily 'Make[s] a recurring protest', but whether or not it is a gesture, vindication or excuse is uncertain as the poem's circular syntax unerringly recurs to the throwaway phrase 'For what it was worth'. Again, MacNeice revives an idiom which must be read simultaneously as a piece of conversational dreck and as an unforgiving tally of what the 'recurring protest' may have been worth; the poem darkly revisits 'The Springboard', where the same phrase had worked to offset the diver's heroism (CP 236).[28] McDonald suggests that 'these poems turn a cruelly cold eye on a generation' through their piteous undermining of overlapping illusions.[29] Yet the poem is not just an indictment of MacNeice's contemporaries. The final section looks to a wider sense of generation:

> As a child showed promise. No need to push him,
> Everyone said. Then came the drought

> And after that, on his twenty-first birthday,
> A cloud no bigger than a god's hand
> And after that there was no need to push him.

The protagonist recalls 'The Slow Starter' from *Solstices*, who defers taking action, with the result that he finds 'his time and talent gone' (*CP* 532–3). The Starter is a victim of his own inertia, his readiness to be seduced by plausible advice like 'Your kind of work is none the worse/ For slow maturing'. In contrast, the progress of the promising child is arrested by nuclear war. 'A cloud no bigger than a god's hand' takes away the need to 'push' the child and, by implication, the rest of humanity. The individual vignettes of 'As In Their Time' culminate in a nightmare image of the dissolution of time and identity. The offhand polish of the individual poems – their seemingly slovenly unrhymed lines and recycled clichés – casually enables the reader to glimpse a possible apocalypse. While apocalyptic had always been a part of MacNeice's writing, arguably it is only with these late poems that the imminence of an ending becomes more tangible than rhetorical.

PARABLE

A week before his death, MacNeice admitted that he 'was taken aback by the high proportion of sombre pieces, ranging from bleak observations to thumbnail nightmares', in *The Burning Perch* (*CP* 795–6). 'Thumbnail nightmare' is a good description of 'As In Their Time', and this comment reflects a change which differentiates the final three volumes from the rest of his oeuvre. Though he had used parable in earlier work, in *Visitations*, *Solstices* and *The Burning Perch* it becomes the predominant mode. Parable does not necessarily entail nightmare, but as the critical study *Varieties of Parable* demonstrates, MacNeice was drawn to texts where the parabolic and the nightmarish are in close proximity. Spenser's *Faerie Queene*, Kafka's *The Castle* and Beckett's plays receive appreciative commentary; it is clear that what MacNeice values in these writers is their ability to give specific shape to the intangible and the troubling. Observing that the 'the terrible enchanter Busirane', who abducts and tortures Amoret in Book III of *The Faerie Queene*, 'is himself a sort of [...] distorted reflection of the love between Amoret and Scudamour', he notes that 'Spenser certainly had the knack of making such reflections solid or [...] of making his abstractions concrete. It is a knack I envy him' (*VP* 112–13). MacNeice displayed something of this knack in his later poems.

Parable had first become important for MacNeice during the 1940s. Though poems like 'Order to View' and 'Christina' precede his work for the BBC, there can be little doubt that it was the need to generate ideas for new radio scripts which stimulated his interest in this kind of writing. Christopher Holme offers a taxonomy of MacNeice's radio plays which identifies a group of these as versions of the quest motif: the perverted quest, the uncertain quest and the false quest.[30] The most celebrated play is *The Dark Tower*, which uses Browning's 'Childe Roland to the Dark Tower Came' as a frame for an existential fantasy. In Holme's terms, this is an uncertain quest: Roland, the protagonist, reluctantly agrees to fulfil his place in a family saga which entails challenging a dragon he will not defeat; as he puts it at the end of the play, 'I Roland, the black sheep, the unbeliever –/ Who never did anything of his own free will –/ Will do this now to bequeath free will to others' (*Plays*, 148). *The Dark Tower* is both MacNeice's finest play and a quest narrative which he continued to explore through the rest of his BBC career. Later plays such as *Prisoner's Progress*, *The Queen of Air and Darkness* and *The Mad Islands* (a fantasia on Irish mythology) all centre on ambiguous, 'unbelieving' protagonists whose stories are more symbolic than naturalistic. As *Varieties of Parable* clarifies, MacNeice felt that 'realism in the photographic sense is almost played out and no longer satisfies our needs' (*VP* 26). Parable plays like *The Dark Tower* and *He Had a Date* force listeners away from the conventions of realism to accept fantastic and schematic narratives with a symbolic undertow. The Dragon in *The Dark Tower* is a comprehensive symbol of evil, which evokes the struggle against fascism. At one point, Blind Peter vividly describes what happens when the Dragon goes unchallenged: 'There was just a kind of a bad smell in the air/ And everything went sour [...]/ And when I looked in the mirror that first morning/ The mirror said "Informer"!' (*Plays*, 125). *The Dark Tower*, as a post-war text, reinforces the position of *Springboard* that the Dragon of fascism must be continuously challenged.

Yet there are significant differences between parable plays and poems. In a radio play, symbolism must be relatively unambiguous so that listeners can grasp most of what is at issue on a single hearing; short poems are not fettered by the same restraints. This points to the generic difficulty of discussing parable and the way in which the term overlaps with competing categories. *Varieties of Parable* shows MacNeice's awareness of such debates: 'I don't like the word "parable" and it suggests something much too narrow for my purpose, namely the parables of the New Testament'. He uses it because the alternatives are even more unsatisfactory; nevertheless, symbol-ism, allegory, fable and myth 'can be squeezed under the umbrella of "parable"' (*VP* 1–2). *Varieties of Parable*'s termino-logical vagueness is useful because it indicates the 'umbrella' of styles MacNeice was seeking to emulate:

> What I myself would now like to write, if I could, would be double-level poetry, of the type of Wordsworth's 'Resolution and Independence', and, secondly, more overt parable poems in a line of descent both from folk ballads such as 'True Thomas' and some of George Herbert's allegories in miniature such as 'Redemption'. (*VP* 8)

Readers of MacNeice's later poems need to be alert to the fact that parable is a consciously loose term which describes a range of practices, genres and modes, connected by their resistance to realism. '[D]ouble-level poetry' offers a more accurate or at least protean category; McDonald's characterization of MacNeicean parable as 'both an unfinished idiom and one which is of itself unfinishable' responds well to the blend of familiarity, sugges-tiveness and menace MacNeice evokes in *Varieties of Parable*.[31] As parable cannot be clearly defined, so *Visitations*, *Solstices* and *The Burning Perch* include texts which may or may not overlap with parable; the greater freedom of these late volumes lies partly in the promiscuous mixing of styles and genres. As we have seen, the sectional poems develop from the experimentalism of the early 1950s and could be used biographically ('Nature Notes') or parabolically ('As In Their Time'). Similarly, these volumes include travel poems, a genre MacNeice had worked on throughout his career. 'Beni Hasan', 'Half Truth from Cape Town' and 'Ravenna' are poetic postcards and reflections on identity, politics and history. 'Beni Hasan' shows the speaker realizing his own ageing, 'It came to me on the Nile that my passport lied/ Calling me dark who am grey', while 'Old Masters Abroad' laconically records the cultural imperialism of the exportation of 'the singing birds of unknown England' through Africa and Asia: 'It is overtime now for the Old Masters' (CP 506, 558). Ostensibly, texts like 'Figure of Eight', 'Hold Up', 'The Truisms' and 'The Taxis' show MacNeice at his most directly parabolic. Though the experiences may derive from events in the poet's life, they are presented as self-enclosed fictions which take place in a universe of symbolic transactions. Nevertheless, they can each be read also as travel poems: each subject is in motion, in the process of a journey which may or may not turn out well.

'Figure of Eight' (CP 516–17) from Visitations shows parable at its most straightforward. MacNeice juxtaposes the emotions of a man on two contrasting journeys. In the first stanza, he is on a bus, 'eager to meet his fate' in the shape of a date who doesn't turn up: 'Though dead on time, to the meeting place agreed,/ But there was no one there'. The poetic register is starkly unadorned, yet, like 'As In Their Time', slangy and truistic phrases are freighted with menace. This becomes explicit in the second stanza, as being 'dead on time' shifts from stale metaphor to bleak certainty:

> Whereas today in the rear and gloom of a train,
> Loath, loath to meet his fate, he cowers and prays
> For some last-minute hitch, some unheard-of abdication,
> But, winding up the black thread of his days,
> The wheels roll on and make it all too plain
> Who will be there to meet him at the station.

As so often, MacNeice expertly conjures the ambience of a train journey, but here the realism of 'the rear and gloom of a train' is held in suspension by the sense that the journey is allegorical. 'Figure of Eight' forensically captures the terror of dying. It is only with the repeated 'Loath, loath to meet his fate' that the text gives away any emotion, yet this twelve-line poem encapsulates the life of a man at two critical phases. Through its focus on different kinds of anticipation, 'Figure of Eight' is an inventive meditation on the inevitability of death, where the protagonist is, much like Roland or Tom Varney, another Everyman in transit.

Like so many of these later poems, 'Figure of Eight' is a poem of returning: both in stanzaic structure and title, it underlines the circularity of experience. *Ten Burnt Offering*'s 'Day of Returning', which blends and reworks the stories of Odysseus and Jacob, introduced this concern on a mythopoeic level. 'Figure of Eight' more credibly explores the dynamics of return in the context of the familiar and the everyday. The suspension of Odysseus in 'Day of Returning' – in the third section he speaks from Calypso's island, hankering for a lover with 'wrinkles to match my own' and for 'someone to argue with/ About my rights of grazing' – anticipates the condition of many of MacNeice's later protagonists (*CP* 357–8). As usual, homecoming is seldom unproblematic. 'Soap Suds' converts a nostalgic return to 'the big/ House he visited when he was eight' into a nightmare which erodes the comfort of nostalgia (*CP* 577). 'The Truisms' (*CP* 565) reworks the parable of the Prodigal Son to show a man reanimating the language and beliefs of a long dead father, concluding with an image pitched between benediction and horror:

> He raised his hands and blessed his home;
> The truisms flew and perched on his shoulders
> And a tall tree sprouted from his father's grave.
>
> (*CP* 565)

Though usually viewed as a poem of achieved reconcilement,[32] 'The Truisms' remains unsettling in that it configures the son seamlessly reoccupying his father's place. The tall tree is a Freudian symbol of the father's posthumous potency and the son's subjection to that power; unlike *A Hope for Poetry*, this retelling of the parable is equivocal.[33] The truisms are an ambiguous patrimony – 'His father gave him a box of truisms/ Shaped like a coffin' – which in their turn shape and reorder the son's values. MacNeice's linguistic vigilance implies that, though we inevitably speak through other people's language through the currency of clichés, this process can erode independence and personality. As early as 1935, 'Homage to Clichés' had both relished and repudiated 'This whole delightful world of cliché and refrain' (*CP* 68). 'The Truisms' in turn connects linguistic convention with emotional commitment in an ultimately disturbing parable.

These poems of homecoming are underpinned by images of suspension. In other texts, this becomes a more general predicament. 'After the Crash', which surrealistically evokes the dislocation of a motorbike rider after crashing, ends as the biker realises 'It was too late to die' (CP 586). In 'Charon', the classical ferryman of dead souls is relocated from Lethe to the Thames in a 'dissolving' London, to warn 'If you want to die you will have to pay for it' (CP 593). The resolution of death which the protagonist of 'Figure of Eight' so much dreads becomes inaccessible. What makes these poems so convincing is their complex amalgam of the real with the surreal. And as experience is suspended, so is language. 'Hold-Up' (CP 561-2) is framed by the simple observation of the first line: 'The lights were red, refused to change'. The rest of the poem moves out from the road block into a portrayal of a petrified society:

> The papers faded in their hands,
> The bubbles in the football pools
> Went flat, the hot news froze, the dates
> They could not keep were dropped like charred
> Matches, the girls no longer flagged
> Their sex, besides the code was lost

Such poetry depends on a sensitivity to what is latent in conversational English. By treating a simple metaphor like 'hot news' literally, MacNeice estranges and revitalizes ordinary language. If the 'code' of sex is lost, the code of the poem invites the reader to accept a language in which words are shifting and unstable from line to line. This linguistic and imagistic surrealism has connections with Science Fiction as well as Spenser and Kafka. MacNeice admired John Wyndham, the writer of *The Day of the Triffids*, and these urban apocalypses exemplify the use MacNeice made of Wyndham's techniques.[34] Horrific images like 'a tall glass box/ On the pavement held a corpse in pickle/ His ear cocked' are a kind of poetic Science Fiction, in which the suspension of the corpse in pickling fluid encapsulates the idea of a society in stasis. By the end of the poem, the repeated phrase 'refused to change' conveys a communal malaise: the people of 'Hold-Up' are frozen partly because of their broader lack of daring.

Nevertheless, the most resonant parables are those which evoke, yet undermine, individual experience. 'The Taxis' (CP

127

583–4) is one of the most celebrated of these poems; Paul Muldoon rightly calls it 'his 1961 masterpiece' and uses its enigmatic refrain as a subtitle for part of his quizzical literary history of Ireland.[35] The poem takes the form of four different taxi rides. Although experience is not suspended, the form of the poem works to undermine narrative coherence:

> In the first taxi he was alone tra-la,
> No extras on the clock. He tipped ninepence
> But the cabby, while he thanked him, looked askance
> As though to suggest someone had bummed a ride.
>
> In the second taxi he was alone tra-la
> But the clock showed sixpence extra; he tipped according
> And the cabby from out his muffler said: 'Make sure
> You have left nothing behind tra-la between you'.

Longley observes that 'The Taxis' 'subverts what at first appears a traditionally straightforward refrain, just as the journey itself becomes weirder'; indeed, 'tra-la' begins as though it is simply a 'folk-ghost', a meaningless intensifier which fills out a line of a song.[36] Yet it becomes the most distinctive part of the poem's code, infecting the cabby's conversation and spilling from line ends into the body of the text. Far from being rhythmic filler, the refrain takes on a totemic significance which enhances the reader's bewilderment. In the final stanza, MacNeice chops 'alone/ Tra-la' across two lines to emphasize its ambiguous discursive force:

> As for the fourth taxi, he was alone
> Tra-la when he hailed it but the cabby looked
> Through him and said: 'I can't tra-la well take
> So many people, not to speak of the dog.'

At one level, 'The Taxis' explores the shortfall between self-perception and social reality. On each ride, the protagonist feels himself to be alone, yet the earthy voice of the cabby insists that he is never alone. As Muldoon suggests, this is another poem of the 'fractured self' as individual and communal identities are confused in the poem's different registers.[37] The refrain conveys some of this tension: is it possible to be properly 'alone' in the idiom of folk songs and nursery rhymes, where phrases like 'tra-la' betray the social and communicative contexts in which such texts are rehearsed and performed?

And yet 'The Taxis' remains a pre-eminently literary text, a modern poem rather than a traditional song, which is silently read by individual readers, 'alone/ Tra-la'. Like many of the poems in *Solstices* and *The Burning Perch*, it points both to the individuality of MacNeice's achievement and to the complex social and literary communities in which he worked. Consider one final point of contact between MacNeice and his contemporaries. The variously urbane, demotic and traditional voice of 'The Taxis' recalls the work of Norman Cameron. 'Nostalgia for Death' exploits the language of psychology to delineate a fracture in its speaker's make-up:

> Psychologists discovered that Miss B
> Suffered from a split personality.
> She had B-1, B-2, 3, 4 and 5,
> All of them struggling in one body alive.
> [...]
> I have, at least, N-1, N-2, N-3.
> N-1 is a glutton, N-2 is a miser,
> N-3 is different, but not much wiser.
> Well, that's enough of that. What of N-O?
> That's the N I'd really like to know.[38]

Cameron uses psychological vocabulary to mock modish accounts of personality disorder. More subtly, these symbols are an estranging device which undermines the speaker and suggests the impossibility of ever really being able to know another person. Like the refrain in 'The Taxis', this pseudo-technical nomenclature darkly replaces more satisfying or comprehensive accounts of personality. Similarly, 'The Taxis' points to the possibility of multiple identities and the difficulty of establishing a coherent narrative. These discontinuous taxi rides and case notes participate in a broader sceptical literary history at the heart of twentieth-century poetry, where language, metaphor and identity are held in a dynamic suspension which, like 'The Snowman', 'will pass'.

Afterword: 'To speak of an end is to begin'

MacNeice's premature death provoked an outpouring of tribute and elegy. He was mourned by his elders and juniors alike. Eliot distinguished him from his contemporaries, insisting 'He had the Irishman's unfailing ear for the music of verse, and he never published a line that is not good reading'.[1] Larkin identified key qualities in MacNeice's writing which made him an attractive model for a younger generation of poets: his status as a 'town observer', and his absorption in 'our everyday life', as well as his sensitivity to 'the crucifying memory, the chance irrevocably lost', in the later work.[2] On a different level, the American poets Robert Lowell and John Berryman wrote elegies which are part of their long sequences *History* and *The Dream Songs*. Lowell's poem translates the ambience of MacNeice's childhood into a characteristically Lowellian idiom: 'A dozen children would visit half a dozen;/ downstairs a lost child bullied the piano'.[3] For Berryman, 'Louis' was 'the lovely man', yet 'was not the character of myth', having to be told about 'Leigh-Mallory's/ remark: "Because it is there"' which would eventually find its way into *Autumn Sequel* to explain 'why/ Men should climb Everest' (*CP* 384).[4]

MacNeice's colleagues and contemporaries offered more intimate portraits of him. Auden gave the address at his memorial service in October 1963, which pays generous tribute to his qualities as a man as well as a poet. A year later, 'The Cave of Making' configures MacNeice as a congenial friend and an ally in poetry as an 'unpopular art' which 'stubbornly still insists upon/ being read or ignored'.[5] Anthony Thwaite's 'For Louis MacNeice' offers a snapshot of MacNeice at the BBC in the later

130

1950s, which conveys the awe the young poet felt for the older man.[6]

In contrast, Spender, who had always had a difficult relationship with MacNeice, delayed producing a poem wholly about him until the late 1970s.[7] 'Louis MacNeice' is a haunting and unsentimental poem which frankly depicts him as a cryptic and bewildering acquaintance with the power to humiliate. Spender's MacNeice 'half-beckoned you up into his high mind/ For a shared view of your clumsiness –/ I mean, me, of mine' (*NCP* 322). Spender's humiliation is compounded in the poem by the text of 'Bagpipe Music', which encapsulates his inability to grapple with either the work or the personality of his dead contemporary:

> Now, reading his poem 'Bagpipe Music', I don't know
>   how to pronounce
> C-e-i-l-i-d-h – nor what it means –
> He looks down from high heaven
> The mocking eyes search-lighting
> My ignorance again.

'Louis MacNeice' is an important poem, not just for its avoidance of conventional elegiac decorum, but also because in this detail it underlines the cultural distance between MacNeice and Spender. By focusing on the word 'Ceilidh', Spender emphasizes MacNeice's Gaelic origins at the expense of his own by implication 'ignorant' Anglocentric perspective.[8] As such, the poem recognizes MacNeice as an Irish poet and points to his growing profile in Irish literary history. This was also anticipated by W. R. Rodgers, whose elegy 'A Last Word' juxtaposes a burial in an Irish landscape with a light prediction of posthumous fame. In Rodgers's view, inspite of his death, MacNeice remains such a prodigious maker that 'to speak of an end/ Is to begin'.[9]

For a generation of younger Irish poets, MacNeice has become a touchstone of artistic authenticity and non-partisan commitment. Seamus Heaney, Michael Longley, Derek Mahon, Tom Paulin and Paul Muldoon have repeatedly flagged their admiration for MacNeice. Mahon's elegy 'In Carrowdore Churchyard' is the archetypal text, in which MacNeice functions as a poetic and moral exemplar: 'This, you implied, is how we ought to live –/ The ironical, loving crush of roses against snow,/

Each fragile, solving ambiguity'.[10] It is important to stress, however, that Mahon's MacNeice is an edited figure – the poet of 'Snow' rather than of *Autumn Journal*.[11] In this context, Muldoon's '7, Middagh Street' is significant because, in ventriloquizing MacNeice in the early 1940s, Muldoon pays a more ample tribute to MacNeice as an internationalist, a poet of progressive political commitment:

> Lorca
> was riddled with bullets
>
> and lay mouth-down
> in the fickle shadow of his own blood.
> As the drunken soldiers of the *Gypsy Ballads*
> started back for town
>
> they heard him calling through the mist,
> 'When I die leave the balcony shutters open.'
> For poetry *can* make things happen –
> not only can, but *must* – [12]

In a brilliant piece of poetic sleight of hand, Muldoon imitates MacNeice in the act of evoking the execution of Lorca as a way of dissenting from Auden's recantation, 'poetry makes nothing happen' in 'In Memory of W. B. Yeats'.[13] For Muldoon–MacNeice, poetry is inherently politically engaged, as in the bitter irony of Lorca being killed by precisely the kind of people he had given voice to in his own works. Similarly, Paulin's *The Invasion Handbook*, a poem which reimagines the events which led up to the Second World War, samples the refrain 'I am not yet born' from 'Prayer Before Birth' to evoke all those who would be adversely affected by the Treaty of Versailles.[14] For both Muldoon and Paulin, MacNeice's Irishness enhances the political character of his work and its engagement with the major upheavals of the twentieth century.

In this book, I have tried to balance a sense of MacNeice as an individual poet with consideration of the ways in which his work is shaped by generational contexts. His complex Irishness, I have suggested, coexists with his consistent revulsion from fascism and his determination during the 1940s to work alongside his British friends and colleagues against what he later represented as the Dragon. Alongside this concern with political context, I have tried to read MacNeice in terms he would have understood: as a writer of variously subtle, demanding, entertaining and moving texts which are in their own shifting terms variously and continuously concerned with the art of poetry and the complicated joys of poetic utterance. The paradoxical qualities of MacNeice's writing – its seesaw between the conversational and the rhetorical, its unsettled, questioning, but never quiescent relationship to issues of commitment – ensured its relevance to a wide number of poets and readers. There is no reason to think this will not continue.

Notes

INTRODUCTION: 'OUR END IS LIFE'

1. M. Harrison and C. Stuart-Clark (eds), *The New Dragon Book of Verse* (Oxford: Oxford University Press, 1977), 4–53; 'Thalassa' is on p. 31.
2. Paul Muldoon, '7, Middagh Street', in *Poems 1968–1998* (London: Faber and Faber, 2001), 173–93.
3. James Elroy Flecker, 'The Old Ships', in Harrison and Clark (eds), *The New Dragon Book of Verse*, 43.
4. Robyn Marsack, *The Cave of Making: The Poetry of Louis MacNeice* (Oxford: Clarendon, 1982), 158 n.7.
5. Ibid., 150.
6. Samuel Hynes, *The Auden Generation: Literature and Politics in England in the 1930s* (1976; repr. London: Pimlico, 1992); Valentine Cunningham, *British Writers of the Thirties* (Oxford: Clarendon, 1988).
7. Edna Longley, *Louis MacNeice: A Critical Study* (London: Faber and Faber, 1988; repr., 1996); Peter McDonald, *Louis MacNeice: The Poet in his Contexts* (Oxford: Clarendon, 1991).
8. Terence Brown, 'MacNeice and the Puritan Tradition', in *Louis MacNeice and his Influence*, ed. K. Devine and A. J. Peacock (Gerrards Cross: Colin Smythe, 1998), 28, 31.
9. In the previous day's *Listener*, however, MacNeice welcomed Auden's *The Oxford Book of Light Verse* as 'one of the most delightful anthologies in English' (*SLC* 99). See 62 below.
10. Ian Hamilton, *Against Oblivion: Some Lives of the Twentieth-Century Poets* (London: Viking, 2002), 178, xiii. See also P. McDonald, *Serious Poetry: Form and Authority from Yeats to Hill* (Oxford: Clarendon Press, 2002), 105.
11. See Hamilton, *Against Oblivion*, xiv–xvi, where he mentions among others George Barker, Basil Bunting, Walter de la Mare, Laurie Lee. I am thinking of poets like Norman Cameron (included by Hamilton: see also ch. 5 below), Ruthven Todd, Bernard Spencer, Charles Madge, David Gascoyne and Clere Parsons. Most of these

writers are represented in Robin Skelton's still influential anthology, *Poetry of the Thirties* (London: Penguin, 1964).

12. Quoted in Jon Stallworthy, *Louis MacNeice* (London: Faber and Faber, 1995), 484.

13. Dodds offset this by dating individual poems as far as he possibly could (*CPD* xvi), a strategy which McDonald has not needed to follow.

CHAPTER 1. MacNEICE AND THE MODERN EVERYMAN

1. W. H. Auden, *The Dyer's Hand and Other Essays* (London: Faber and Faber, 1963), xi.

2. Robin Skelton (ed.), *Poetry of the Thirties*, 30.

3. W. H. Auden, *Prose and Travel Books in Prose and Verse*, vol. 1, *1926–1938*, ed. E. Mendelson (London: Faber and Faber, 1996), 434, 436. Auden, like MacNeice echoes the rejection of esoteric poetry in Michael Roberts's *New Signatures* (1932), quoted later in this chapter. See ch. 3 below.

4. W. H. Auden and Christopher Isherwood, *Plays and Other Dramatic Writings by W. H. Auden: 1928–1938*, ed. E. Mendelson (London: Faber and Faber, 1989), 318.

5. Percy Bysshe Shelley, *Shelley's Poetry and Prose: Authoritative Texts and Criticism*, ed. D. H. Reiman and S. B. Powers (New York: Norton, 1977), 508; T. S. Eliot, *Selected Essays* (London: Faber and Faber, 1932; 3rd edn, 1951), 289.

6. Christopher Caudwell, *Illusion and Reality: A Study of the Sources of Poetry* (1937; repr. London: Lawrence & Wishart, 1977). MacNeice's italics paraphrase a formulation Caudwell uses on pp. 36 and 141. Caudwell became a hero of the literary left after dying in Spain while fighting for the International Brigade in February 1937.

7. Iona and Peter Opie (eds), *The Oxford Dictionary of Nursery Rhymes* (Oxford: Clarendon, 1951), 337–8.

8. The information in this section is based on Jon Stallworthy's biography, *Louis MacNeice*.

9. Auden, *Prose and Travel Books in Prose and Verse*, vol. 1, 59. The phrase 'fine old tradition' recalls Auden's poem 'Our hunting fathers', which contrasts the values of the fathers with an emergent revolt against 'that fine tradition' (Auden, *The English Auden*, ed. E. Mendelson (London: Faber and Faber, 1977), 151).

10. Day Lewis disassembled the contents of 'A Time to Dance' in subsequent editions, and this lyric became a free-standing poem entitled 'A Carol' (*CPDL* 196).

11. See 'Traveller's Return' (*Prose*, 83–91). During 1940, Auden and Isherwood were criticized for their emigration by friends and enemies alike in the British press; for a sympathetic account of the furore, see Peter Parker, *Isherwood: A Life* (London: Picador, 2004), 456–63.

12. Stallworthy records that several of MacNeice's friends believed that 'he volunteered for service in the Royal Navy, but was rejected on grounds of bad eyesight' (*Louis MacNeice*, 287, 522).

13. Ibid., 330.

14. *The Mad Islands* and *The Administrator* (1964); *Persons from Porlock and Other Plays for Radio* (1969); *Selected Plays of Louis MacNeice* (1993) reprints several of the more famous radio plays (*Christopher Columbus*; *The Dark Tower*) alongside previously unpublished scripts (*He Had a Date*; *Prisoner's Progress*).

15. See Barbara Coulton, *Louis MacNeice in the BBC* (London: Faber and Faber, 1980), 36–77.

16. Stallworthy, *Louis MacNeice*, 451.

17. Iona and Peter Opie (eds), *Nursery Rhymes*, 265–7. The first verse of the rhyme is: 'Lavender's blue, diddle, diddle,/ Lavender's green;/ When I am king, diddle, diddle,/ You shall be queen'. MacNeice quotes these lines in *Prisoner's Progress*, where it is sung by Catsmeat (*Plays*, 168).

18. Information on Day Lewis and Spender is drawn from Sean Day-Lewis, *C. Day-Lewis: An English Literary Life* (London: Weidenfeld and Nicolson, 1980) and John Sutherland, *Stephen Spender: The Authorized Biography* (London: Viking, 2004).

19. Quoted in Albert Gelpi, *Living in Time: the Poetry of C. Day Lewis* (New York: Oxford University Press, 1998), 13–14.

20. C. Day Lewis, *The Buried Day* (London: Chatto and Windus, 1960), 217.

21. See my essay, '"Your Thoughts Make Shape Like Snow": Louis MacNeice on Stephen Spender', *Twentieth-Century Literature*, 48:3 (2002), 292–323, for a detailed account of their relationship.

22. My emphasis.

23. Stephen Spender, 'Chapter X of *Instead of Death*', *Oxford Poetry*, 11:1 (2000), 26. For MacNeice's comment that this fiction said more about 'Stephen's lust to mythologise the world in which he walked' than Auden, see *The Strings are False*, 128.

24. Roy Campbell, *Talking Bronco* (London: Faber and Faber, 1946), 79, 81.

25. Stephen Spender, *Forward from Liberalism* (London: Gollancz, 1937), 7.

26. On Auden's politics, see Stan Smith, *W. H. Auden* (Plymouth: Northcote House, 1997), 10.

27. Michael Roberts (ed.), *New Signatures* (London: Hogarth Press, 1932), 12, 14. *New Signatures* and *New Country* include the work of other poets (not all of whom conform to Roberts's diagnosis): Julian Bell, Richard Eberhart, William Empson, John Lehmann, William Plomer, A. S. J. Tessimond, Richard Goodman, Charles Madge and Rex Warner.

28. Sean Day-Lewis, *C. Day-Lewis*, 77.

29. McDonald, *Louis MacNeice*, 15.

30. Stephen Spender, 'Mr. MacNeice's Poems', *New Verse*, 17 (October–November 1935), 18.

31. See MacNeice's 'Autobiographical Sketch', drafted in the early 1940s and updated in 1955: 'Politics: distrust all parties but consider capitalism must go' (*Prose*, 72).

32. *A Time to Dance* also includes 'The Ecstatic', which echoes both Shelley's 'To a Skylark' and Hopkins's 'The Windhover' and recuperates an almost completely traditional poetic idiom, describing a skylark as 'Buoyed, embayed in heaven's noon-wide reaches –/ For soon light's tide will turn – Oh stay!' (*TD* 25).

33. Day Lewis, *The Buried Day*, 181–207. Day Lewis later became a reader for Chatto & Windus, working there 'on a strictly part-time basis'; see Peter Stanford, *C Day-Lewis: A Life* (London: Continuum, 2007), 219.

CHAPTER 2. MODERN HOPES: THE POETRY OF THE 1930s

1. For a revisionist reading of the poem, see my 'The Poetry of the 1930s' in *Aestheticism and Modernism: Debating Twentieth-Century Literature*, ed. R. D. Brown and S. Gupta (Abingdon and Milton Keynes: Routledge in association with the Open University, 2005), 184–6.

2. Hynes, *The Auden Generation*; Bernard Bergonzi, *Reading the Thirties: Texts and Contexts* (London: Macmillan, 1978); Cunningham, *British Writers of the Thirties*; Adrian Caesar, *Dividing Lines: Poetry, Class and Ideology in the 1930s* (Manchester: Manchester University Press, 1991).

3. Terence Brown, *Louis MacNeice: Sceptical Vision* (Dublin: Gill and Macmillan, 1975), 10.

4. Hynes, *The Auden Generation*, 334; McDonald, *Louis MacNeice*, 203.

5. Brown, 'MacNeice and the Puritan Tradition', 31.

6. Longley, 'MacNeice and After', *Poetry Review*, 78:2 (1988), 6.

7. Hynes, *The Auden Generation*, 160.

8. Auden, *The English Auden*, 299.

9. For challenges to the idea that Auden became increasingly conservative, see Stan Smith's Introduction in *The Cambridge Companion to W. H. Auden*, ed. S. Smith (Cambridge: Cambridge University Press, 2004), 12.

10. *A Hope for Poetry* was first published in 1934 (3rd edn with Postscript, 1936). *The Destructive Element* and 'Poetry To-day' were both first published in 1935, the latter in Geoffrey Grigson's *The Arts To-day*, which also included Auden's 'Psychology and Art To-day'. Though less well known than *Modern Poetry*, the views expressed in 'Poetry To-day' are congruent with those of the later work.

11. C. Day Lewis, 'Letter to a Young Revolutionary', in *New Country: Prose and Poetry by the Authors of 'New Signatures'*, ed. M. Roberts (London: Hogarth Press, 1933), 41.

12. See James Reeves (ed.), *Georgian Poetry* (Harmondsworth: Penguin, 1962), xi–xxiii.

13. See 12 above.

14. Stephen Spender, 'Poetry and Revolution', in *New Country*, 62, 66, 71.

15. C. Day Lewis, 'Revolutionaries and Poetry', repr. in *Writing the Revolution: Cultural Criticism from 'Left Review'*, ed. D. Margolies (London: Pluto Press, 1998), 57, 58.

16. See Gelpi, *Living in Time*, 50.

17. George Orwell, 'Inside the Whale', in *The Collected Essays, Journalism and Letters of George Orwell*, vol. 1, *An Age Like This 1920–1940*, ed. S. Orwell and I. Angus (Harmondsworth: Penguin, 1970), 561. Though the object of Orwell's scorn was actually Auden, the poem which he quotes, 'You'll be leaving soon and it's up to you, boys' (Orwell garbles this as 'You're leaving now, and it's up to you boys') is from Day Lewis's *The Magnetic Mountain*; see *The Complete Poems of C. Day Lewis*, 144.

18. My emphases.

19. My emphases.

20. Michael O'Neill and Gareth Reeves, *Auden, MacNeice, Spender: The Thirties Poetry* (Basingstoke: Macmillan, 1992), 61.

21. Julian Symons, from '"A Communist to Others": A Symposium', in *Auden, 'The Map of all my Youth': Early Works, Friends, and Influences*, ed. K. Bucknell and N. Jenkins (Clarendon: Oxford, 1990), 178.

22. O'Neill and Reeves, *Auden, MacNeice, Spender*, 126.

23. Auden, *The English Auden*, 212.

24. See Sutherland, *Stephen Spender*, 147.

25. Ibid., 173.

26. Ibid., 172.

27. Hynes, *The Auden Generation*, 145.

28. Auden, *The English Auden*, 59. See also Hynes, *The Auden Generation*, 32.
29. Hynes, *The Auden Generation*, 148.
30. See Marsack, *The Cave of Making*, 7–8; Longley, *Louis MacNeice*, 43–4.
31. Compare 'Letter to W. H. Auden': 'it is a blessing to our generation, though one in the eye for Bloomsbury, that you discharged into poetry the subject-matters of psycho-analysis, politics and economics' (*SLC* 83).
32. McDonald, *Louis MacNeice*, 18.
33. John Bunyan, *The Pilgrim's Progress*, ed. W. R. Owens (Oxford: Oxford University Press, 2003), 88. For MacNeice's wider debt to Bunyan, see my 'Everyman's Progresses: Louis MacNeice's Dialogues with Bunyan', in *Reception, Appropriation, Recollection: Bunyan's Pilgrim's Progress*, ed. W. R. Owens and S. Sim (Oxford: Peter Lang, 2007), 147–63.
34. For an analysis of the relationship between 'After they have tired of the brilliance of cities' and 'To a Communist', see my '"Your Thoughts Make Shape Like Snow"', 306–12.
35. *Louis MacNeice Reads a Selection of his own Poetry*, broadcast 26 August 1949, produced by Frank Hauser. Script in the BBC Written Archives, 2.
36. Compare Auden's 'Letter to William Coldstream, Esq.': 'We'd scrapped Significant Form, and voted for Subject' (*LI* 222).
37. McDonald, *Louis MacNeice*, 56.

CHAPTER 3. A GRAIN OF SALT: THE LATER 1930s

1. Hynes, *The Auden Generation*, 242. On Spain, see Paul Preston, *A Concise History of the Spanish Civil War* (London: Fontana, 1996).
2. For Spender's Spanish Civil War poetry, see *The Still Centre* (*NCP* 114–23), which includes determinedly anti-heroic poems such as 'Port Bou' and 'Ultima Ratio Regum'. In these texts, it is the technology of modern warfare rather than fascism per se which has become the real enemy.
3. Auden, *The English Auden*, 48–9. See also Stan Smith, 'Auden's Light and Serio-comic Verse', in *The Cambridge Companion to W. H. Auden*, ed. S. Smith (Cambridge: Cambridge University Press, 2004), 100–101.
4. Auden, *Prose and Travel Books in Prose and Verse*, vol. 1, 431–2.
5. Ibid., 436.
6. See Cunningham, *British Writers of the Thirties*, 211–40, for a summary of this debate.

7. Auden, *The English Auden*, 214–15. MacNeice may have been thinking of Auden's 'Johnny', a poem which centres on a less obviously 'bourgeois' couple; see *The English Auden*, 213.

8. See Auden, *As I Walked Out One Evening: Songs, Ballads, Lullabies, Limericks and Other Light Verse*, ed. E. Mendelson (London: Faber and Faber, 1995), which collects Auden's lighter work throughout his career.

9. See Auden, *Prose and Travel Books in Prose and Verse*, vol. 1, 772.

10. See Marsha Bryant, 'Auden and the "Arctic Stare": Documentary as Public Collage in *Letters From Iceland*', *Journal of Modern Literature*, 17:4 (1991), 537–65, which minimizes MacNeice's contribution to the text, other than as the subject of Auden's photographs.

11. See the photos 'Leaving Hraensnef', 'The Student of Prose and Conduct', 'Horses on Lava', 'The Motorboat cost 40 Kronur' and 'Louis' (*LI*, facing pp. 5, 32, 157, 224, 225).

12. See Bryant, 'Auden and the "Arctic Stare"', for a critical reading of Auden's photographs in the context of the volume's broader democratizing commitments.

13. Compare 'Dialogue in Stornoway': 'Qu'allez vous faire dans cette galère? [...] Just a spot of belles-lettres, my dear' (*ICM* 33).

14. For MacNeice's comic contemporary defence of vulgarity, see *Selected Prose of Louis MacNeice*, 43–4.

15. 'Life of Lord Leverhulme' was reprinted for the American *Poems 1925–1940*. The title comes from this volume; in *I Crossed the Minch*, it is just headed as the second part of the 'Potted History' chapter. See also *Collected Poems of Louis MacNeice*, 754–9.

16. Quoted in Stallworthy, *Louis MacNeice*, 212.

17. See Stallworthy, *Louis MacNeice*, 252.

18. Longley, *Louis MacNeice*, 59.

19. William T. McKinnon, *Apollo's Blended Dream: A Study of the Poetry of Louis MacNeice* (London: Oxford University Press, 1971), 159; McDonald, *Louis MacNeice*, 86.

20. Hynes, *The Auden Generation*, 372, 370.

21. Longley, *Louis MacNeice*, 57.

22. In an essay of 1949, MacNeice noted, 'after *Autumn Journal* I tired of journalism' (*SLC* 161).

23. Compare Caesar, *Dividing Lines*, 101, with Edna Longley, '"Something Wrong Somewhere?": MacNeice as Critic', in *Louis MacNeice and his Influence*, ed. Devine and Peacock, 67.

24. See Richard R. Bozorth, *Auden's Games of Knowledge: Poetry and the Meanings of Homosexuality* (New York: Columbia University Press, 2001), 154–5.

25. Smith, 'Auden's Light and Serio-comic Verse', 103.

26. O'Neill and Reeves, *Auden, MacNeice, Spender*, 186.

27. Quoted in Marsack, *The Cave of Making*, 43.
28. See Bozorth, *Auden's Games of Knowledge*, 134.
29. McDonald, *Louis MacNeice*, 88; my emphasis. See also Marsack, *The Cave of Making*, 45.
30. Quoted in Marsack, *The Cave of Making*, 43.
31. For 'Take away this cup', see Mark 14:36; for 'Lord, I am not worthy', see Matthew 8:8.
32. Philip Larkin, 'Louis MacNeice', in *Further Requirements: Interviews, Broadcasts, Statements and Book Reviews*, ed. A. Thwaite (London: Faber and Faber, 2002), 18.
33. Philip Larkin, *Collected Poems*, ed. A. Thwaite (London: Marvell Press and Faber and Faber, 1990), 111.

CHAPTER 4. SO WHAT AND WHAT MATTER? POETRY AND WARTIME

1. See Horace, *Odes III: Dulce Periculum*, ed. and trans. D. West (Oxford: Oxford University Press, 2002), 258–61. MacNeice's poem begins with Horace's phrase 'aere perennius' ('more lasting than bronze') from *Odes* 3.30. For more on MacNeice and fame, see McDonald, *Serious Poetry*, ch. 7, 'MacNeice's Posterity'.
2. Christopher Isherwood, *Christopher and his Kind* (1st edn 1976; Minneapolis: University of Minnesota Press, 2001), 333.
3. See 20–1 above.
4. Longley, *Louis MacNeice*, 28; see also McDonald, *Louis MacNeice*, 1–9, 203–29, and Fran Brearton, *The Great War in Irish Poetry: W. B. Yeats to Michael Longley* (Oxford: Oxford University Press, 2000), 116–50, for the argument that MacNeice revisits the Great War in ways subtly different from his English contemporaries, and Heather Clark, 'Revising MacNeice', *Cambridge Quarterly*, 31:1 (2002), 77–92, for consideration of the ways in which Seamus Heaney, Michael Longley and Derek Mahon have read MacNeice.
5. Paul Muldoon (ed.), *The Faber Book of Contemporary Irish Poetry* (London: Faber and Faber, 1986), 81–144; see also the volume's Prologue, which reproduces a broadcast discussion between MacNeice and F. R. Higgins from 1939, in which MacNeice repudiates Higgins's contention that 'you, as an Irishman, cannot escape from your blood': 'I think one may have such a thing as one's racial blood-music, but that, like one's unconscious, it may be left to take care of itself' (18).
6. The fullest version is in *The Last Ditch*, where it runs to ten poems. *Plant and Phantom* reduced this to seven, while *Collected Poems 1925–*

1948 cut a further two and changed the title to 'The Closing Album'. See *Collected Poems* (ed. McDonald), 803.

7. For a fuller consideration of *The Poetry of W. B. Yeats*, see my 'Neutrality and Commitment: MacNeice, Yeats, Ireland and the Second World War', *Journal of Modern Literature*, 28:3 (2005), 109–29, and Brearton, *The Great War in Irish Poetry*, 140–7.

8. Stallworthy, *Louis MacNeice*, 260.

9. Quoted in Kate Whitehead, *The Third Programme: A Literary History* (Oxford: Clarendon, 1989), 111.

10. MacNeice, *Black Gallery: No.10 Adolf Hitler*, 16 July 1942. Script in BBC Written Archives (WAC Script 4), 1.

11. Clark, 'Revising MacNeice', 92; see pp. 83–92 for a judicious reading of MacNeice's wartime work which stresses MacNeice's commitment to the Allied cause and solidarity with Londoners during the Blitz.

12. Peter McDonald, 'Louis MacNeice: Irony and Responsibility', in *The Cambridge Companion to Contemporary Irish Poetry*, ed. M. Campbell (Cambridge: Cambridge University Press, 2003), 63.

13. The poems are: 'Littoral', 'The Cromlech', 'Carrick Revisited', 'Slum Song', 'The Strand', 'Last Before America', 'Western Landscape' and 'Under the Mountain'. They were included in *Holes in the Sky* (1948) where they are printed in this order, which McDonald's *Collected Poems* has restored; see 259–68.

14. McDonald's *Collected Poems* reads, 'But the black will remain to draw the hearses' (p. 263), a misreading (deriving from Dodds's *Collected Poems*, 225) since in both *Collected Poems 1925–1948* and *Eighty-Five Poems*, MacNeice retained the plural 'blacks'.

15. See also Brearton, *The Great War in Irish Poetry*, 125–9.

16. McDonald, *Louis MacNeice*, 217.

17. See also 'Twelfth Night' and 'The Stygian Banks', both of which are prompted by Shakespearean allusions (CP 255–6, 282–95).

18. Clark, 'Revising MacNeice', 78. Muldoon's *Faber Book of Contemporary Irish Verse* includes only two poems from *Springboard*, neither of which centrally addresses the conflict (112–14).

19. Stallworthy, *Louis MacNeice*, 329.

20. For summaries, see Valentine Cunningham (ed.), *The Penguin Book of Spanish Civil War Verse* (Harmondsworth: Penguin, 1980), 70–1, and my 'The Poetry of the 1930s', in *Aestheticism and Modernism*, ed. Brown and Gupta, 191–4.

21. Genesis 11:1–9.

22. MacNeice may have borrowed this technique from George Herbert, who uses unrhymed lines to devastating effect in poems like 'Deniall'. Herbert's presence in *Springboard* is signalled by the use of a phrase from 'Providence' as the epigraph to the first part of the collection: 'Even poisons praise thee' (*S.* 9). For MacNeice on

Herbert, see *Selected Literary Criticism of Louis MacNeice*, 175–80, and *Varieties of Parable*, 46–7, 50. See Marsack, *The Cave of Making*, 113–15, for a suggestive comparison of 'Prayer Before Birth' with Herbert's 'Sighs and Grones'.

23. Caudwell, *Illusion and Reality*, 36; see 12 above and *Selected Literary Criticism of Louis MacNeice*, 122, 145, for contemporaneous citations.
24. See note 22 above.
25. For discussion of the BBC work, see Coulton, *Louis MacNeice and the BBC*; Christopher Holme, 'The Radio Drama of Louis MacNeice', in *British Radio Drama*, ed. J. Drakakis (Cambridge: Cambridge University Press, 1981), 37–71; Whitehead, *The Third Programme*, 70–2, 121–2; Alan Heuser, 'Tracing MacNeice's Development in Drama: A Commentary on the Published and Unpublished Plays', in *Louis MacNeice and his Influence*, ed. Devine and Peacock, 133–55. Alan J. Peacock's 'Louis MacNeice: Transmitting Horace', *Revista alicantina de estudios ingleses*, 5 (1992), 119–30, discusses the unpublished play *Carpe Diem* (1956). MacNeice's unpublished radio scripts are held at the BBC Written Archives Centre at Caversham.
26. First broadcast by the Home Service on 28 June 1944, then revived for the Third Programme on 14 February 1949. The second version was the more successful production, and this is the version printed in *Plays*.
27. Quoted in Clark, 'Revising MacNeice', 84.
28. MacNeice's other major radio features tend to feature similar kinds of hero. See in particular *The Dark Tower*, *Prisoner's Progress* and the unpublished *Queen of Air and Darkness*.
29. See Stallworthy, *Louis MacNeice*, 321–2, and my response in 'Neutrality and Commitment', 123–5.
30. See Terence Brown, *Louis MacNeice: Sceptical Vision*, 31–45, for a reading of MacNeice's poetry of childhood in relation to Romanticism; for repression in 'Autobiography', see my '"Your Thoughts Make Shape Like Snow"', 294–5.

CHAPTER 5. WAITING FOR THE THAW: THE LATER MACNEICE

1. Though now more famous as a commuter town with an upwardly mobile football club, Reading used to be the home of the biscuit manufacturers Huntley & Palmer.
2. See McKinnon, *Apollo's Blended Dream*, 47 and note 3.
3. MacNeice's sister, Elizabeth Nicholson, notes the significance Christmas continued to have for him throughout his life: 'to the

end of his life he tried year after year to recreate the spirit of those early Rectory Christmases, often, I am afraid, sad because he never quite could'; see 'Trees Were Green', in *Time Was Away: The World of Louis MacNeice*, ed. T. Brown and A. Reid (Dublin: Dolmen Press, 1974), 12.

4. MacNeice, *Selected Poems*, ed. W. H. Auden (London: Faber and Faber, 1964), 9. See also MacNeice, *Selected Poems*, ed. M. Longley (London: Faber and Faber, 1988), xxi.

5. Longley, *Louis MacNeice*, 114.

6. John Montague, 'Despair and Delight', in *Time Was Away*, ed. Brown and Reid, 123; McDonald, *Louis MacNeice*, 130–53.

7. Fraser came to prominence as a spokesman for the 'New Apocalypse' poets during the early 1940s, a movement for which MacNeice felt some contempt (*SLC* 141–2). His relationship with MacNeice was evidently collegial and faintly hostile: see 'Evasive Honesty: The Poetry of Louis MacNeice', in *Vision and Rhetoric: Studies in Modern Poetry* (London: Faber and Faber, 1959), esp. 179–80.

8. See *OED*, 'non-U' and Kate Fox, *Watching the English: The Hidden Rules of English Behaviour* (London: Hodder, 2004), 75–6.

9. See also the 1949 essay, 'Poetry, the Public, and the Critic' (*SLC* 164–9).

10. On Cameron, see Warren Hope, *Norman Cameron: His Life, Work and Letters* (London: Greenwich Exchange, 2000), and Norman Cameron, *Collected Poems and Selected Translations*, ed. W. Hope and J. Barker (London: Anvil, 1990).

11. For Spender, see Hope, *Norman Cameron*, 80. For surveys which include Cameron, see A. T. Tolley, *The Poetry of the Thirties* (London: Gollancz, 1975), 211–14, and Caesar, *Dividing Lines*, 131–4.

12. In Cameron, *Collected Poems*, 18, 17. Intriguingly, Larkin seems to have been unaware or unimpressed by Cameron; see Hamilton, *Against Oblivion*, 147.

13. See Stallworthy, *Louis MacNeice*, 487, for a guide to the 'dramatis personae' of *Autumn Sequel*.

14. Hope, *Norman Cameron*, 128 and *passim*. Cameron died on 20 April 1953, which could be construed as 'This summer' from the autumn vantage of MacNeice's poem.

15. McDonald, *Louis MacNeice*, 148–9.

16. Longley, *Louis MacNeice*, 115.

17. McDonald, *Louis MacNeice*, 148. For MacNeice's use of *terza rima*, see Steve Ellis, 'Dante and Louis MacNeice: A Sequel to the *Commedia*', in *Dante's Modern Afterlife: Reception and Response from Blake to Heaney*, ed. N. Havely (Basingstoke: Macmillan, 1998).

18. McDonald, *Louis MacNeice*, 150.

19. Helen Gardner (ed.), *The New Oxford Book of English Verse 1250–1950* (Oxford: Oxford University Press, 1972), 21–2, 944–5. MacNeice's knowledge of Dunbar is shown by his use of the refrain of 'To the City of London' (often attributed to Dunbar) in 'Goodbye to London': 'Nevertheless let the petals fall/ Fast from the flower of cities all' (*CP* 608–9).

20. Quoted in Stallworthy, *Louis MacNeice*, 411.

21. MacNeice's interest would have been stimulated by Spender's translation; see Rainer Maria Rilke, *Duino Elegies*, trans. J. B. Leishmann and Stephen Spender (London: Hogarth, 1939).

22. Longley, *Louis MacNeice*, 115.

23. Iona and Peter Opie (eds), *The Oxford Dictionary of Nursery Rhymes*, 229–32. For 'jack', see *OED*, n.1 2 a, and compare Shakespeare: 'Since every Jack became a gentleman/There's many a gentle person made a jack' in *King Richard III*, ed. Antony Hammond (London: Methuen, 1981), 155.

24. My emphases.

25. See *OED*, dree, v. 2 c.

26. At about the time of writing this poem, MacNeice planned a book in which landscape was to be the frame for autobiography; see *The Strings are False*, 14, 216–38.

27. See Fraser, 'Evasive Honesty', 181–2. MacNeice's attitude is shown by the stage play *One for the Grave*, where Common Sense is introduced as a delusive vamp: 'you dressed me up as Common Sense. But underneath of course […] I was your Wishful Thinking' (*Plays*, 216).

28. See 100 above.

29. McDonald, *Louis MacNeice*, 194. See *One for the Grave* for another parodic version of this phrase in a popular song (*Plays*, 208).

30. Holme, 'The Radio Drama of Louis MacNeice', 63–4.

31. McDonald, *Louis MacNeice*, 176.

32. See, for example, Stallworthy, *Louis MacNeice*, 446–7, and my response in 'MacNeice in Fairy Land', in *Edmund Spenser: New and Renewed Directions*, ed. J. B. Lethbridge (Madison: Fairleigh Dickinson University Press, 2006), 362–8.

33. See 35–6 above.

34. See *Varieties of Parable*, 26 and *Selected Literary Criticism of Louis MacNeice*, 233–4.

35. Paul Muldoon, *To Ireland, I* (Oxford: Oxford University Press, 2000), 94.

36. Longley, *Louis MacNeice*, 166.

37. Muldoon, *To Ireland, I*, 94.

38. Cameron, *Collected Poems*, 60. See also Hope, *Norman Cameron*, 7–10.

AFTERWORD: 'TO SPEAK OF AN END IS TO BEGIN'

1. T. S. Eliot, 'Mr Louis MacNeice', *The Times*, 5 September 1963, 14.
2. Larkin, *Further Requirements*, 18.
3. Robert Lowell, 'Louis MacNeice 1907–63', in *Collected Poems*, ed. F. Bidart and D. Gewanter (London: Faber and Faber, 2003), 538. See also *The Letters of Robert Lowell*, ed. S. Hamilton (New York: Farrar, Straus and Giroux, 2005), 436.
4. John Berryman, 'Dream Song 267', in *The Dream Songs* (London: Faber and Faber, 1990), 286.
5. Auden, 'A Memorial Address', in *Time Was Away*, ed. Brown and Reid, 5–10; 'The Cave of Making', in *Collected Poems*, ed. E. Mendelson (London: Faber and Faber, 1976), 521–5.
6. In Brown and Reid (eds), *Time Was Away*, 111–12.
7. Though dated in *New Collected Poems* to 1985, Spender had published a version of the poem with a different title in *The Thirties and After* (1978). The earlier 'One More New Botched Beginning' briefly elegizes MacNeice alongside Bernard Spencer (*NCP*, 307–9).
8. For more on the implications of this poem, see my '"Your Thoughts Make Shape Like Snow"', 315–17.
9. W. R. Rodgers, 'A Last Word', in *Collected Poems* (London: Oxford University Press, 1971), 144.
10. Derek Mahon, 'In Carrowdore Churchyard', in *Selected Poems* (London: Penguin, 1993), 11.
11. See Clark, 'Revising MacNeice', 80; Richard York, 'Louis MacNeice and Derek Mahon', in *Louis MacNeice and his Influence*, ed. Devine and Peacock, 89–90; and Brearton, *The Great War in Irish Poetry*, 147–50, 216.
12. Muldoon, *Poems 1968–1998*, 192.
13. Auden, *The English Auden*, 242.
14. Tom Paulin, *The Invasion Handbook* (London: Faber and Faber, 2002), 5.

Select Bibliography

WORKS BY LOUIS MacNEICE

(Except where otherwise indicated, MacNeice's work is published in London by Faber and Faber.)

Collections

Poems 1925–1940 (New York: Random House, 1940).
Collected Poems 1925–1948 (1949).
Eighty-Five Poems (1959).
Selected Poems, ed. W. H. Auden (1964).
Collected Poems, ed. E. R. Dodds (1966; 1979).
Selected Literary Criticism of Louis MacNeice, ed. Alan Heuser (Oxford: Clarendon, 1987).
Selected Poems, ed. Michael Longley (1988).
Selected Prose of Louis MacNeice, ed. Alan Heuser (Oxford: Clarendon, 1990).
Selected Plays of Louis MacNeice, ed. Alan Heuser and Peter McDonald (Oxford: Clarendon, 1993).
Collected Poems, ed. Peter McDonald (2007).

Individual volumes

Blind Fireworks (London: Gollancz, 1929).
Poems (1935).
The Agamemnon of Aeschylus (1936).
Letters from Iceland (with W. H. Auden) (1937).
Out of the Picture (1937).
The Earth Compels (1938).
I Crossed the Minch (London: Longmans, Green and Co, 1938).
Modern Poetry: A Personal Essay (Oxford: Oxford University Press, 1938).
Zoo (London: Michael Joseph, 1938).
Autumn Journal (1939).

147

The Last Ditch (Dublin: Cuala, 1940; repr. Shannon: Irish University Press, 1971).

Plant and Phantom (1941).

The Poetry of W. B. Yeats (Oxford: Oxford University Press, 1941; repr. London: Faber and Faber, 1967).

Christopher Columbus (1944).

Springboard: Poems 1941–1944 (1944).

The Dark Tower and Other Radio Scripts (1947).

Holes in the Sky (1948).

Ten Burnt Offerings (1952).

Autumn Sequel: A Rhetorical Poem in XXVI Cantos (1954).

Visitations (1957).

Solstices (1961).

The Burning Perch (1963).

The Mad Islands and *The Administrator* (1964).

The Strings are False: An Unfinished Autobiography, ed. E. R. Dodds (1965).

Varieties of Parable (1965).

Persons from Porlock and Other Plays for Radio (London: BBC, 1969).

Unpublished works

All unpublished radio scripts quoted in the text are held at the BBC Written Archives at Caversham. For fuller bibliographies, see Barbara Coulton, *Louis MacNeice in the BBC*; and Alan Heuser, 'Tracing MacNeice's Development in Drama'.

Black Gallery: No.10 Adolf Hitler (1942).

Louis MacNeice Reads a Selection of his own Poetry (1949).

The Queen of Air and Darkness: A Study in Evil (1949).

Carpe Diem (1956).

WORKS BY MacNEICE'S CONTEMPORARIES

Auden, W. H., *The Dyer's Hand and Other Essays* (London: Faber and Faber, 1963).

—— *Collected Poems*, ed. Edward Mendelson (London: Faber and Faber, 1976).

—— *The English Auden*, ed. Edward Mendelson (London: Faber and Faber, 1977).

—— *As I Walked Out One Evening: Songs, Ballads, Lullabies, Limericks and Other Light Verse*, ed. Edward Mendelson (London: Faber and Faber, 1995).

—— *Prose and Travel Books in Prose and Verse*, vol. 1, *1926–1938*, ed.

Edward Mendelson (London: Faber and Faber, 1996).

—— *Prose*, vol. 2, *1939–1948*, ed. Edward Mendelson (London: Faber and Faber, 2002).

—— and Christopher Isherwood, *Plays and Other Dramatic Writings by W. H. Auden: 1928–1938*, ed. Edward Mendelson (London: Faber and Faber, 1989).

Cameron, Norman, *Collected Poems and Selected Translations*, ed. Warren Hope and Jonathan Barker (London: Anvil, 1990).

Caudwell, Christopher, *Illusion and Reality: A Study of the Sources of Poetry* (1937; repr. London: Lawrence & Wishart, 1977).

Day Lewis, C., *A Hope for Poetry* (Oxford: Blackwell, 1934; 1936).

—— *A Time to Dance and Other Poems* (London: Hogarth, 1935).

—— *The Buried Day* (London: Chatto and Windus, 1960).

—— *The Complete Poems of C. Day Lewis* (Stanford: Stanford University Press, 1992).

Isherwood, Christopher, *Christopher and his Kind* (1976; repr. Minneapolis: University of Minnesota Press, 2001).

Spender, Stephen, *The Destructive Element: A Study of Modern Writers and Beliefs* (London: Jonathan Cape, 1935).

—— *Forward from Liberalism* (London: Gollancz, 1937).

—— *World within World: The Autobiography of Stephen Spender* (London: Faber and Faber, 1951).

—— *New Collected Poems*, ed. Michael Brett (London: Faber and Faber, 2004).

ANTHOLOGIES

Auden, W. H. (ed.), *The Oxford Book of Light Verse* (Oxford: Clarendon, 1938).

Cunningham, Valentine (ed.), *The Penguin Book of Spanish Civil War Verse* (Harmondsworth: Penguin, 1980).

Muldoon, Paul (ed.), *The Faber Book of Contemporary Irish Poetry* (London: Faber and Faber, 1986).

Roberts, Michael (ed.), *New Signatures: Poems by Several Hands* (London: Hogarth, 1932).

—— *New Country: Prose and Poetry by the Authors of 'New Signatures'* (London: Hogarth, 1933).

Skelton, Robin (ed.), *Poetry of the Thirties* (London: Penguin, 1964; repr. 2000).

BIBLIOGRAPHICAL AND BIOGRAPHICAL STUDIES

Armitage, C. M., and Neil Clark, *A Bibliography of the Works of Louis MacNeice* (London: Kaye and Ward, 1973).

Coulton, Barbara, *Louis MacNeice in the BBC* (London: Faber and Faber, 1980).

Day-Lewis, Sean, *C. Day-Lewis: An English Literary Life* (London: Weidenfeld and Nicolson, 1980).

Heuser, Alan, 'Tracing MacNeice's Development in Drama: A Commentary on the Published and Unpublished Plays', in Devine and Peacock, *Louis MacNeice and his Influence*.

Hope, Warren, *Norman Cameron: His Life, Work and Letters* (London: Greenwich Exchange, 2000).

Stallworthy, Jon, *Louis MacNeice* (London: Faber and Faber, 1995).

Stanford, Peter, *C Day-Lewis: A Life* (London: Continuum, 2007).

Sutherland, John, *Stephen Spender: The Authorized Biography* (London: Viking, 2004).

CRITICAL STUDIES

Bergonzi, Bernard, *Reading the Thirties: Texts and Contexts* (London: Macmillan, 1978).

Brearton, Fran, *The Great War in Irish Poetry: W. B. Yeats to Michael Longley* (Oxford: Oxford University Press, 2000; pbk, 2003).

Brown, Richard Danson, '"Your Thoughts Make Shape Like Snow": Louis MacNeice on Stephen Spender', *Twentieth-Century Literature*, 48:3 (2002), 292–323.

—— 'Neutrality and Commitment: MacNeice, Yeats, Ireland and the Second World War', *Journal of Modern Literature* 28:3 (2005), 109–29.

—— 'The Poetry of the 1930s' in *Aestheticism and Modernism: Debating Twentieth-Century Literature 1900–1960*, ed. Richard Danson Brown and Suman Gupta (London: Routledge, 2005).

—— 'MacNeice in Fairy Land' in *Edmund Spenser: New and Renewed Directions*, ed. J. B. Lethbridge (Madison: Fairleigh Dickinson University Press, 2006).

—— 'Everyman's Progresses: Louis MacNeice's Dialogues with Bunyan' in *Reception, Appropriation, Recollection: Bunyan's 'Pilgrim's Progress'*, ed. W. R. Owens and Stuart Sim (Oxford: Peter Lang, 2007).

Brown, Terence, *Louis MacNeice: Sceptical Vision* (Dublin: Gill and Macmillan, 1975).

—— 'MacNeice and the Puritan Tradition', in Devine and Peacock,

Louis MacNeice and his Influence.

—— and Alec Reid (eds), *Time Was Away: The World of Louis MacNeice* (Dublin: Dolmen, 1974).

Caesar, Adrian, *Dividing Lines: Poetry, Class and Ideology in the 1930s* (Manchester: Manchester University Press, 1991).

Clark, Heather, 'Revising MacNeice', *Cambridge Quarterly*, 31:1 (2002), 77–92.

Cunningham, Valentine, *British Writers of the Thirties* (Oxford: Clarendon, 1988).

Devine, Kathleen and Alan J. Peacock (eds), *Louis MacNeice and his Influence* (Gerrards Cross: Colin Smythe, 1998).

Gelpi, Albert, *Living in Time: The Poetry of C. Day Lewis* (New York: Oxford University Press, 1998).

Goodby, John, *Irish Poetry since 1950: From Stillness into History* (Manchester: Manchester University Press, 2000).

Haberer, Adolphe, *Louis MacNeice, 1907–1963: L'homme et la poésie* (Bordeaux: Presses Universitaires de Bordeaux, 1986).

Hamilton, Ian, *Against Oblivion: Some Lives of the Twentieth-Century Poets* (London: Viking, 2002).

Holme, Christopher, 'The Radio Drama of Louis MacNeice', in *British Radio Drama*, ed. John Drakakis (Cambridge: Cambridge University Press, 1981).

Hynes, Samuel, *The Auden Generation: Literature and Politics in England in the 1930s* (London: Bodley Head, 1976; repr. London: Pimlico, 1992).

Longley, Edna, 'MacNeice and After', *Poetry Review* 78:2 (1988), 6–10.

—— *Louis MacNeice: A Critical Study* (London: Faber and Faber, 1988; repr. 1996).

—— '"Something Wrong Somewhere?": MacNeice as Critic', in Devine and Peacock, *Louis MacNeice and his Influence*.

Marsack, Robyn, *The Cave of Making: The Poetry of Louis MacNeice* (Oxford: Clarendon, 1982).

McDonald, Peter, *Louis MacNeice: The Poet in his Contexts* (Oxford: Clarendon, 1991).

—— *Serious Poetry: Form and Authority from Yeats to Hill* (Oxford: Clarendon Press, 2002).

—— 'Louis MacNeice: Irony and Responsibility', in *The Cambridge Companion to Contemporary Irish Poetry*, ed. Matthew Campbell (Cambridge: Cambridge University Press, 2003).

McKinnon, William T., *Apollo's Blended Dream: A Study of the Poetry of Louis MacNeice* (London: Oxford University Press, 1971).

Moore, D. B., *The Poetry of Louis MacNeice* (Leicester: University of Leicester Press, 1972).

O' Neill, Michael, and Gareth Reeves, *Auden, MacNeice, Spender: The Thirties Poetry* (Basingstoke: Macmillan, 1992).

Poster, Jem, *The Thirties Poets* (Buckingham: Open University Press, 1993).

Press, John, *Louis MacNeice* (London: British Council with the National Book League and Longmans, Green & Co., 1965).

Tolley, A. T., *The Poetry of the Thirties* (London: Gollancz, 1975).

Welch, Robert, 'Yeats and MacNeice: A Night-Seminar with Francis Stuart', in Devine and Peacock, *Louis MacNeice and his Influence*.

Whitehead, John, *A Commentary on the Poetry of W. H. Auden, C. Day Lewis, Louis MacNeice, and Stephen Spender* (Lewiston, NY: E. Mellen Press, 1992).

Whitehead, Kate, *The Third Programme: A Literary History* (Oxford: Clarendon, 1989).

Index

Lightning Source UK Ltd.
Milton Keynes UK
UKOW03f0016130614

233317UK00001B/19/P